Endorsements by Global Christian Leaders

DR. MARK BELILES HAS BEEN ACTIVE  TERS,
AND OTHER POLITICIANS OF MANY C
CONSULTING, AND HOLDING SEMINA
TEACH IN MY OWN CHURCH (HALLELU   J
HAVING COOPERATED WITH HIM FOR   ..., CONNECTIONS, I
STRONGLY ENDORSE HIS BIBLICAL AND TRANSFORMATIONAL PERSPECTIVES TO
FELLOW-MINISTERS AND EVANGELICAL CULTURAL LEADERS AROUND THE WORLD.
REVD DR. SANG-BOK DAVID KIM, WORLD EVANGELICAL ALLIANCE

DR. MARK BELILES BRINGS MANY YEARS OF EXPERIENCE, EFFECTIVENESS,
INTEGRITY AND CLARITY TO THE CHALLENGE OF CREATIVE CULTURAL CHANGE
BASED ON THE FOUNDATIONAL PRECEPTS THAT CULTURE MATTERS AND IDEAS
HAVE CONSEQUENCES.
LUIS BUSH, TRANSFORM WORLD CONNECTIONS

WE STRONGLY PROMOTE AND SHARE THE LIFE-CHANGING BOOKS AND
TEACHINGS OF MARK BELILES AT OUR CONFERENCES SO THAT CHRISTIANS MAY
OBTAIN THE KNOWLEDGE OF THEIR CHRISTIAN HERITAGE AND EXPERIENCE THE
TRANSFORMING EFFECT OF IT IN THEIR LIVES AND THEIR NATION.
JOYCE AND DAVE MEYER, JOYCE MEYER MINISTRIES

I HAVE HEARD MARK BELILES TEACH AND FIND HIS MESSAGE IS VITAL FOR THE
CHURCH IF SHE IS GOING TO TAKE HER COMMISSION TO DISCIPLE NATIONS
SERIOUSLY.
DARROW MILLER, CO-FOUNDER, DISCIPLE NATIONS ALLIANCE

DEMONS POSSESS INDIVIDUALS. SATAN IS OUT TO DECEIVE NATIONS. WHO WILL
CRUSH SATAN'S HEAD UNDER HER FEET? IF GOD WAS GOING TO DO THAT, HE
COULD HAVE DONE IT IN THE GARDEN OF EDEN OR IN THE WILDERNESS WHEN
SATAN TRIED TO TEMPT GOD THE SON. GOD SAID TO THE ANCIENT SERPENT
THAT HE WOULD EMPOWER EVE'S SEED FOR DEALING WITH THE SUPERNATURAL
EVIL. MARK BELIES SHOWS HOW YOUR CHURCH CAN CRUSH THE EVIL
CORRUPTING YOUR NATION.
VISHAL MANGALWADI, AUTHOR, THIS BOOK CHANGED EVERYTHING

DR. MARK BELILES IS A TRANSFORMATION PRACTITIONER WITH AN AMAZING TRACK RECORD OF IMPACTING HIGH LEVEL LEADERS AND NATIONS! HIS SCHOLARLY THEOLOGICAL AND HISTORICAL WORK COMBINED WITH HIS VAST EXPERIENCE IN THE FIELD, ENABLES HIM TO WRITE ON THIS SUBJECT LIKE FEW CAN. I HIGHLY RECOMMEND THIS AND ALL HIS BOOKS!
JOSEPH MATTERA, U. S. COALITION OF APOSTOLIC LEADERS

I HAVE KNOWN AND WORKED CLOSELY WITH DR. MARK BELILES FOR MANY YEARS, INCLUDING WITH HIS WORK AT BOTH THE PROVIDENCE FOUNDATION AND THE AMERICAN TRANSFORMATION COMPANY (ATC). FOR PASTORS AND LEADERS IN ANY OF THE SEVEN SPHERES OF CULTURAL INFLUENCE WHO DESIRE TO TRANSFORM THEIR COMMUNITIES IN A STRATEGIC AND BIBLICAL MANNER, I RECOMMEND ATC AND THEIR RESOURCES, INCLUDING RESEARCH, BOOKS, AND SEMINARS.
DAVID BARTON, WALLBUILDERS

DR. MARK BELILES AND THE AMERICA TRANSFORMATION COMPANY IS HELPING PASTORS AND LEADERS IN THEIR LOCAL COMMUNITIES TO REALLY BRING LONG-TERM BIBLICAL TRANSFORMATION OF A NATION. WITH BIBLICAL WORLDVIEW PRINCIPLES AND BEST-PRACTICES CORROBORATED BY PRACTICAL EXAMPLES IN CHURCH HISTORY, A NEW GENERATION OF "PILGRIMS" ARE EMERGING AT THIS CRUCIAL TIME IN OUR NATION. THEIR BOOKS, SEMINARS, ONLINE RESOURCES AND PERSONAL COACHING WILL CERTAINLY HELP YOU BE PART OF RESTORING GOD'S DREAM FOR AMERICA.
JIM GARLOW, CEO, WELL VERSED, FORMER PASTOR, SKYLINE CHURCH

JUST OPEN THE BOOK AND LOOK AT THE TABLE OF CONTENTS. THAT'S ALL IT WILL TAKE TO TELL WHY THIS BOOK [CHRIST'S STRATEGY TO DISCIPLE NATIONS] BY DR. MARK BELILES, IS ONE OF MY ALL TIME FAVORITES. HIS RESEARCH IS BACKED UP BY PERSONAL EXPERIENCE OBSERVING THE SHIFTING BATTLE TERRAIN IN OVER 50 NATIONS. HIS MESSAGE IS REVOLUTIONARY - PRAYER, CHURCH GROWTH AND REVIVAL HAVE NEVER BEEN ENOUGH TO SIGNIFICANTLY TRANSFORM A NATION. THIS IS HERESY TO THOSE WHO DON'T UNDERSTAND WHY AMERICA AND THE WEST IS ON LIFE SUPPORT. LIKE A MASTER SAFE CRACKER MARK HAS LEANED HIS EAR UP AGAINST THE VAULT AND CAREFULLY TURNED THE TUMBLERS OF THE LOCK THIS WAY AND THAT TILL IT WENT "CLICK" AND THE STEEL DOOR OPENED. THERE IS A WEALTH OF INSIGHT INSIDE THE VAULT OF THIS BOOK. WHEN INTERCESSION, REVIVAL AND ACTIVISM MERGE WE WILL SEE CITIES SHAKE (AND APOSTLES LOCKED UP.)
LANCE WALNAU, LANCE WALNAU MINISTRIES

YOUR BOOKS AND TRAINING ARE AN EXCELLENT RESOURCE FOR US. I BELIEVE THE LORD HAS PREPARED YOU OVER THE YEARS TO BE OF ASSISTANCE TO OUR NEW DEMOCRATIC SOUTH AFRICA.
KENNETH MESHOE, MEMBER OF PARLIAMENT, SOUTH AFRICA

DR. MARK BELILES AND THE AMERICA TRANSFORMATION COMPANY IS SHOWING US HOW TO BIBLICALLY RESPOND IN A COMPREHENSIVE AND HISTORICALLY-PROVEN WAY TO TRANSFORM CULTURE FOR CHRIST. AS A PRESBYTERIAN PASTOR IN AMERICA, I ESPECIALLY RECOMMEND THIS MINISTRY AND ITS GREAT BOOKS, SEMINARS, AND RESOURCES. I'M BIASED, BUT I HAD THE PRIVILEGE TO CO-WRITE WITH DR. BELILES ONE OF THOSE BOOKS ON JEFFERSON'S FAITH---OR LACK THEREOF, DOUBTING THOMAS.
JERRY NEWCOMBE, D.MIN., AUTHOR/CO-AUTHOR OF 31 BOOKS, COLUMNIST. D. JAMES KENNEDY MINISTRIES

THERE ARE VERY FEW MINISTRIES THAT ACTUALLY HELP LEADERS IN ALL THE SPHERES OF CULTURE TO ORGANIZE AND DEVELOP LONG-TERM STRATEGIC PLANS FOR DISCIPLING NATIONS. MARK BELILES AND THE AMERICA TRANSFORMATION COMPANY DOES THAT. THROUGH HIS BOOKS, SEMINARS AND COACHING, STATESMEN ARE FORMED AND MOBILIZED FOR EFFECTIVE LEADERSHIP IN AMERICA AND MANY OTHER COUNTRIES. I HIGHLY RECOMMEND HIS WORK FOR SUCH A TIME AS THIS.
DENNIS PEACOCKE, STATESMEN PROJECT

AMERICA IS AN IDEA...A DREAM OF GOD THAT NEEDS REBIRTH IN A NEW GENERATION OF LEADERS. AMERICA TRANSFORMATION COMPANY IS DOING THAT. I HIGHLY RECOMMEND THIS STRATEGIC MINISTRY.
BISHOP HARRY JACKSON, INT'L COMMUNION OF EVANGELICAL CHURCHES

MARK BELILES HAS DEEP UNDERSTANDING AND VALUES OF THE SOCIAL-ECONOMIC AND CULTURAL HERITAGE OF NATIONS. HE BRINGS THE BIBLICAL PERSPECTIVE OF HOW GOD HAD SHAPED THE NATIONS FOR HIS PURPOSE AND GLORY. IN HIS MESSAGES HE STIMULATES THE AUDIENCE TO REFLECT ON THE SPIRITUAL DIMENSION AS WE FACE UP THE CHALLENGE OF TRANSFORMATION OF OUR SOCIETY. HIS WIDE KNOWLEDGE OF THE HISTORICAL AND CULTURAL ROOTS IN THE DEVELOPMENT OF NATIONS HELPS US TO PLAY OUR PART TO TRANSFORM OUR SOCIETY. I WHOLE-HEARTEDLY COMMEND HIM TO YOU.
REVD CANON DR. JAMES WONG, ANGLICAN CHURCH, SINGAPORE

How Nations Cast Out Their Demons

Biblical Best Practices for the Church to Overcome
Cultural Sin and Oppression

Dr. Mark A. Beliles

Global Transformation Network
www.NationalTransformation.com

Global Transformation Network
304 Minor Ridge Rd
Charlottesville, VA 22901
www.NationalTransformation.com
434-249-4032
Email: NationalTransformation@gmail.com
First printing, 2019

Table of Contents

Preface

It may be surprising to some, but there are no examples in history where large numbers of Christians, mega-churches, and so-called "revivals" have completely transformed a nation. An exhaustive study of countries around the world during the two millennia of Christianity confirms that only when such growth includes an intentional strategy to train and place networked teams of leaders in the most influential institutions of culture does Christianity bring significant change in nations. With the ongoing base of prayer and evangelism, God has always used strategically-placed leaders to change the course of nations.

James Davidson Hunter, sociology professor at the University of Virginia in the United States, has confirmed in his book *To Change the World* that Christians must have a strategy for discipling the nation in order for significant transformation to occur. My own study of church history and travel in over 60 nations has proven the reality of Dr. Hunter's observations. Historically, the fundamental best-practices that significantly transformed culture are tasks that are ignored and/or de-emphasized by the modern church.

What are the essential elements needed to disciple a nation? Besides the church, there are six major areas of cultural influence: family, education, arts & media, medicine, business, and government. Earlier writers and thinkers such as the Dutchman Abraham Kuyper spoke of these as "domains" or "spheres" of authority and jurisdiction. Francis Schaeffer, Loren Cunningham, Bill Bright, and others have used similar terms and lists. Other writers and speakers such as C. Peter Wagner, Lance Walnau, and Johnny Enlow have called these the seven "mountains" of culture. In the 1980s my colleague Stephen McDowell and I began teaching about these key cultural areas and published *America's Providential History* and *Liberating the Nations* to that end.

Various emerging movements in many nations have started to embrace and apply these historic strategies. Luis Bush serves a movement called Transform World. Discipling Nations Alliance is led by Darrow Miller and Bob Moffat. Dennis Peacocke leads the Statesmen Project, and John Kelly the International Coalition of Apostolic Leaders. The Global Transformation Network that I have the privilege to serve-and its American branch known as America Transformation Company are working in similar ways. May this book assist the church in renovating the kingdoms of this world into "the kingdoms of our Lord and of His Christ" (Revelation 11:15).

Introduction

Many books explain the importance of prayer, evangelism, and planting churches. To bring full transformation and reformation to a nation, the hearts of the people must indeed be transformed. Personal repentance and conversion are where all godly change begins. But after God changes the hearts of men, what then? When God transforms men, their families, businesses, schools, churches, neighborhoods, towns, cities, states, and nations should see the effects of that change. But this does not always happen today.

The Apostle Paul wrote, "where the Spirit of the Lord is, there is liberty" (2 Cor 3:17). When the gospel enters a man's heart, a new source of authority is established for determining decisions and establishing values. Discipleship is necessary however to teach man how to apply the revealed truth of Jesus Christ to every area of his life. Likewise, as the gospel is infused in the life of a nation, the potential for national change is enhanced. For successful outcomes though, a strategy must be in place to see true transformation in every area of society. How can we create such a strategy? We must begin by looking at the truths of Scripture and the remarkable examples that history affords us of the church's best-practices.

The Mission of the Church

In the Great Commission found at the end of the Gospels, Jesus clearly defines the church's purpose: "go . . .and make disciples of all the nations" (Matthew 28:19). In the historic church that first transformed pagan Europe into a Christian culture, they understood this mission. Places of worship, churches, cathedrals were not built for several centuries. Instead their primary focus was on building people for significant impact. These people would become ambassadors of another kingdom sent by the church to every sphere of national life: family, education, arts & media, medicine, business, and government.

Too often today, the measurement of pastoral success is numerical growth, and the constant construction of new buildings in which to house growing congregations. A mega-church is the ultimate attainment. Accomplishment is measured by the amount of activities and events that fill up church calendars even though these rarely relate to transforming culture. These measurements of success in the modern church are non-existent in the New Testament. Jesus himself and all the Apostles would have been criticized as failures by this criteria. No one built a church building and membership in their fellowship was small.

The Church's Main Purpose and Responsibilities:

As an institution, it is useful first to summarize the main functions of a church:

- Gather the people of God for worship, the Lord's Supper, baptism, prayer, and the proclamation of the Truth (Acts 2:42; 1 Cor 11:23-26; 14:26; 1 Tim 4:13-16).
- Instruct God's people in Biblical truth. This involves Sunday preaching, regular classes, and other educational opportunities (2 Tim 3:16-17).
- Equip and mobilize God's people for service (Eph 4:11-12,16; Titus 3:8,14). The church must also provide coordination and support for individuals and families in their mission.

Most everyone agrees with these functions, but what is important to discuss is the scope of the instruction and equipping. Today it is mostly on personal and church life, but historically the church did this for every sphere of life. This led to creation of advanced schools and colleges with departments associated with all the spheres of culture where believers live out their callings.

Christ's Criteria for Measuring Ourselves in the Church

When Jesus gave the mission to go "make disciples of all the nations, he gave the disciples his criteria for measuring success. In the parallel passage of the Great Commission found in Mark 16, we can see that Jesus added "signs" that would follow this mission in which he detailed a way to measure progress of evangelism and discipling nations. He said "those who believe" will:

1. "cast out demons"
2. "speak with new tongues"
3. "take up serpents"
4. "drink anything deadly"
5. "lay hands on the sick"

Many times we read this in a personal manner, but this was part of His commission that clearly references "nations." These signs should be equally applied not only to individuals who believe but to the nations who believe and are disciple effectively.

In the next few chapters we will examine Jesus' first sign for Strategic Discipleship of nations - casting out demons. In other words, solve the spiritual problems.

Chapter 1

CRY OUT: Community-oriented Unified Prayer

Ezek 22:30 **"stand in the breach before me for the land"**
Luke 10:19 **"I have given you authority to tread on serpents"**

2009, Surabaya, Indonesia
Tens of thousands had gathered in the arena. Most were Muslim. But there were clearly many Hindu, Buddhist and Christian people in attendance, each celebrating their part in the history of their nation with cultural expressions in costume, dance, music and art.

Leaders of these different faiths gathered on the platform and I was invited up as a guest. We took hands and at times were arm in arm to pray for Indonesia. Next to me were former radical Imams who previously trained and taught Muslims to attack and harm Christians, burn their churches, and perpetrate mayhem. But now they were praying with me and others for God to come, push back the spiritual darkness of the demons, and deliver us from evil.

This gathering of diverse religious leaders in prayer was the central point of the event. We did not cower or restrain, but we prayed in Jesus' name and worshipped Him. The Muslim religious leaders agreed with us in this. Why? The awesome love of Jesus and His power had been demonstrated to them by many Christians' unrelenting acts of kindness. Jesus had personally revealed Himself to them in dreams and visions. He had healed and touched people of different faiths in undeniable ways. They knew the answer to evil in their nation was to pray together for the city and the nation.

A few years later I joined leaders from around the world who gathered for the World Prayer Assembly. The football (soccer) stadium was filled with 100,000 people. The Muslim vice-president greeted and welcomed those in attendance. It was a historic time. We worshipped, prayed, and interceded for the nations. Our praise and intercession were specifically directed against forces of darkness.

Dr. David Yonggi Cho, who led the largest church in the world located in South Korea, was there praying for the nations. Just a few years earlier, I was at Prayer Mountain in Korea myself, which Dr. Cho had established not just for personal prayer but to raise up prayer for the nation. As I sat in my small cubicle on that mountainside, I could hear the intercessory cries of others surrounding me. No wonder the church had grown so much in Korea and Indonesia.

That "mountain top" experience reminded me of prayer on my face in the mud on the national mall with half a million others in 1980 in Washington, D.C. At Washington for Jesus we cried out to God for change and the affairs in the nation turned. In 1996 on that same mall, several million men gathered to fast and pray, called together by Promise Keepers. My son was with me at that gathering. In my own city, pastors and civic leaders regularly gather at a prayer breakfast and at the house of prayer that I helped to create.

As I stood on that stage in Indonesia I could see the power of God moving in a majority-Muslim country to bring significant transformation and healing that most people would never see on their nightly news broadcast. Thank you Lord for letting me be part of these strategic moments in other lands in addition to your prayer movement in my own the secular sophisticated college town. I can see that regardless of the conditions, when prayer is turned outward in strategic intercession, history is changed.

Pastors and church leaders need a new paradigm to think about how we fulfill our mission in order to shift our focus from solely the congregational needs to discipling our city and nation. When our mission statement includes discipleship of a city and a nation, our priorities change from internal benefits to external expressions. Our worship services and prayer meetings will necessarily be transformed as well.

In the early history of Christianity in Europe, a tiny minority of the population transformed a pagan continent into a Christian culture. This happened because they understood their mission. They did not embark on it by building great cathedrals and places of worship, although there are many of those in Europe today. Their primary focus instead was building people who considered themselves ambassadors of Christ's kingdom to their neighborhood, workplace, and civic activities.

As stated in the introduction, the first purpose and responsibilities of pastors and church leadership are to gather the people of God for worship, the Lord's Supper, prayer, and the proclamation of the Truth. Politicians, militaries, and other institutions have no responsibility to do this. The church alone is uniquely equipped for this purpose.

Prayer and Prophetic Proclamation

In Mark 16, after instructing the church to preach to all creatures and *"make disciples of all nations,"* the first criteria that Jesus describes for evaluating the effectiveness in this mission is that signs like "casting out of demons" would be evident.

A church can measure its success by effectively dealing with the spiritual forces of darkness that are oppressing not just individuals, but people groups and cultures. Paul told the Corinthians to tear down strongholds with the weapons that are mighty through God (2 Cor 10). The Apostle Paul wrote in Ephesians 6 that we do not wrestle merely with flesh and blood in a nation" but against "principalities and powers in the heavenly places." They are the "spiritual forces of darkness."

When Jesus sent out his disciples to preach His word and heal the sick, they returned rejoicing that the demons were subject to them. Jesus responded by explaining to them that as they proclaimed the truth, Satan fell like lightning. Through this, Jesus was showing the disciples how fasting, praying and declaring a biblical message for life benefits the culture.

When Daniel found himself as a refugee in a foreign land and his people dealing with persecution and threats, he began to fast and pray. After three weeks, an angel came to him and told him that although his prayer was heard immediately, the "prince of Persia" stood against the angel and delayed him from coming. This "prince" was not a flesh and blood prince but the spiritual prince assigned to that territory. To complete the break-through that Daniel was asking for his people, the "prince" or demon needed to be defeated. Unfortunately, much of the church does not act out of recognition of the demonic realm. Education about a believer's authority and the existence of the kingdom of darkness is needed to equip us to confront the demons of our culture.

The Importance of Unity with Other Churches
Knowing our adversary is not enough. Christians must fight our opposition in unity with other churches in their area or region. Territorial demons are not cast out in the same manner as individual demons. They are more powerful and entrenched in the culture. It takes unified, informed intercession with other churches in a region to see territorial darkness pushed back and breakthroughs come.

There are some outstanding examples in church history. The church in Jerusalem lifted up its voice together in Acts 4:24-31 and saw great breakthrough. The Irish Celtic church were outstanding in unified prayer. One example was a prayer meeting started by Comgall in the year 555 in Bangor, Ireland that operated 24 hours a day for almost 300 years without stopping! The result was a fully transformed and disciple Christian nation. Another example was in central Europe many centuries later. There in eastern Germany the Moravian Christians started a prayer meeting in 1727 that operated 24 hours a day and lasted about a hundred years without ceasing. The result of that was one of the greatest missionary movements in the history of Christianity, touching many nations. A more modern example is in Korea at a Prayer Mountain that began in 1973 and has had almost non-stop prayer ever since. The 24/7 House of Prayer started in Kansas City in the United States in 1999 and has spread to many places. There are many more prayer movements in history but few have dramatically changed nations for reasons we will examine.

One preparation for unified worship is reconciliation. Every believer is called to mend damaged or broken relationships. In the Sermon on the Mount Jesus said that if we approach God and remember a breach with a brother, we must leave our offering and go to the person to first be reconciled. As believers we need to be more mindful of how our personal behavior, our personal relationships, our interactions, impact the community. Our calling is to serve and not be served for we are more blessed in giving and sacrificing our time and our comfort zones rather than being self-centered and individualistic with our faith.

Corporate divisions between churches of different denominations, between races and classes, as well as generational rifts often harm our communities and prevent true transformation. Unless we recognize the need for unity in the church, we will not see the "signs" follow us of casting out the nation's demons.

The Importance of Information and Research about the Darkness

A church can worship and pray without ever positively influencing culture. To see results, we must make an examination of culture. We have to do spiritual reconnaissance, determine the enemy's strongholds, and pray intelligently against the work of the devil.

The experience of Daniel teaches us that the obstacles to breakthrough in our city and nation must be ascertained. In Chapters 9 & 10 of Daniel he finds himself among God's people in exile living under the rule of pagans. He studies the books of Scripture and analyzes the behavior of the Jews, and proceeds to intercede in that light. It is also important to research the history of the community and the culture and discover the areas where greatest destruction is occurring. Armed with this information and the discernment given through the Holy Spirit, we can fight with more focus and effectiveness. In fact, Daniel discovers that an obstacle to the answer was "the prince of the kingdom of Persia" (Dan 10:13) that first had to be overcome. This was not an earthly prince, but a spiritual power of darkness that was assigned over Persia.

Scripture promises that when the devil is resisted, he will flee. Sometimes Christians fail to resist and fight, asking God to do something when He has already instructed on the methods to fight the darkness. Once our discovery process is accomplished, we must ask God to take captive those demonic forces and bring them into submission. We must stand together and resist the darkness in corporate worship and prayer gatherings. Then, and only then, His original purposes for our communities and countries can be realized.

Repentance and letting go of our own worldview is often needed to truly understand the areas of darkness in our culture. Many times our own preconceived ideas blind us to the true battleground. For example, many Christians are quick to pray against freemasonry or witchcraft in a nation, but neglect the far more pervasive propagation of sinful and demonic ideas and behavior through our school systems where the vast majority of Christian families send their children! We must repent of our old way of thinking and relearn God's principles and best practices from scripture and church history in order to realize what must be done to reclaim our nations.

Learning to Pray for and Proclaim Good Things

Far too often, Christians identify demons, pray against them in their nation, and stop there, thinking the mission is accomplished. But Jesus said unless something more powerful fills the void, the demons will come back even stronger (Matt 12:43-45). Just as in a battle, to push the enemy off a high ground is a waste if the attacking army does not place a strong detachment of the army on that spot. Likewise, it is not enough to simply focus on demons and evil with our prayers. After we cast out the demons, we need to learn to pray for good to come. And we also must seek to actively fill that vacated area with godly things and better leaders.

For a nation or society to stand under pressure, a strong foundation is necessary in every component of society. Any individual, family, church, association, or government with even the weakest foundation may be able resist when the pressure is not overwhelming. However, in the face of the pressures of today, most quickly collapse unless supported with a solid underpinning. It is like a bridge that may work fine for normal weight to cross it. But if a major load attempts to cross it, the bridge may collapse. The ancient Romans built arched stone bridges thousands of years ago that still stand today because they had a strong design. Likewise, for any stability in culture, the structure must be braced by principles and best practices found in the Bible.

To bring reformation to the nations, change must begin internally. Nations seeking to shift from communistic economic systems to a free market or from state control to more self-government must recognize that these goals will never be accomplished unless the people have the proper understanding of character and thought. It is not enough to set up external edifices, even when they have worked in other nations and have been part of the best and most free governments in history. Good structures on weak foundations will still crumble. The best form of government in ill hands can do nothing great or good.

Biblical principles in the hearts of the people form the basis of a "Christian" nation. Building Christian nations means developing thoughts, attitudes, and actions on the Word of God. When this is accomplished first in the individuals, these principles will be manifested in the nation's law and throughout other societal institutions.

Seven Good Things to Pray and Proclaim Over Your Nation

History reveals seven good things that when flourishing in a nation, create a strong, powerful foundation which can hinder evil from advancing. By using these seven areas as a template for prayer in our cities and nations, we can see untapped power for good multiply in our countries.

1. Self-Government

When people hear the word *government,* they usually think of civil government. But this bureaucratic entity, is only one type of government. The word *government* means *direction, regulation, control, restraint.* This can be both internal and external. Internal government, the first and most important type of government, is self-government. When God created Adam and Eve, He did not first initiate civil government; He commanded man to govern himself.

Internal government in the heart must rely on man's ability to govern his conscience, will, character, thoughts, ideas, motives, conviction, attitudes, and desires. How a man governs himself internally affects his external actions, speech, conduct, use of property, etc. Each external sphere of government is a reflection of the internal government. The internal is causative to the external. The type of government that exists in the homes, churches, schools, businesses, associations, or civil realms of a nation is a reflection of the internal or self-government within her citizens.

Hugo Grotius, the seventeenth century Dutch clergyman and scholar who systematized the subject of the Law of Nations, summarized the principle of self-government:

"He knows not how to rule a kingdom, that cannot manage a Province; nor can he wield a Province, that cannot order a City; nor he order a City, that knows not how to regulate a Village; nor he a Village, that cannot guide a Family; nor can that man Govern well a Family that knows not how to Govern himself; neither can any Govern himself unless his reason be Lord, Will and Appetite her

Vassals; nor can Reason rule unless herself be ruled by God, and (wholly) be obedient to Him."

Grotius was clear; you must rule yourself before you can rule others. He reveals how the flow of power should occur within a country, from the internal to the external. The following chart summarizes the idea.

Increasing Levels of Responsibility:

Kingdom
Province
City
Village
Family
Self
Reason
Will
Appetite

The Bible teaches that rulers must be self-governed. We can see this in Paul's criteria for leaders in the church. It is important that he "manages his own household well, keeping his children under control with all dignity (but if a man does not know how to manage his own household, how will he take care of the church of God?)" (1 Timothy 3:4-5).

Many civil government leaders today attempt to govern their nation, yet are unable to effectively direct and control their own lives or their families. They are divorced or living in adultery. They have children breaking laws and living wildly. They have businesses that violate regulations or fail to pay taxes, etc. These men and women should be replaced by those who can rule their own lives. Real power come from within: "He who is slow to anger is better than the mighty, and he who rules his spirit, than he who captures a city" (Proverbs 16:32). Effective government can begin only when citizens learn to govern themselves.

The more internal and self-governing a people are, the less external government is needed. Consequently, the more external rules and laws required to maintain civilian control reflects the diminishing amount of self-government. For instance, in some countries it is a law that every citizen must vote. If a person does not care and is not informed, what value is such a law?

History teaches that man can control himself with limited success. In world history, it was apparent in ancient Greek democracies that were short-lived, and in modern totalitarian regimes rarely does a ruler restrain himself and finally a violent overthrow takes place. Since self-government cannot be externally imposed, another source for internal control is needed.

Grotius reveals that man can only be self-governed if his reason, will, and appetite are ruled by God. Self-control is based on-obedience to the Creator and His standards of conduct. The fourth President of the United States and chief architect of the U.S. Constitution, James Madison, stated that the founders of America chose "...*to rest all our political experiments on the capacity of mankind for self-government."*

As people become less self-governed, and give up more and more of the power that ought to be theirs, the civil government (primarily the national government) will grow, make more laws (many outside its realm of jurisdiction), and impose external laws on what was meant to be governed internally. Lack of self-government leads to greater centralized external government, resulting in the loss of individual liberty. In the entire Bible there are about 11,000 words, but in just one recent law under President Obama in the USA there were 11,000,000 words!

Pray for more self-government in your nation's people and leaders. Prophetically proclaim for it to emerge.

2. Voluntary Union

The people of a free nation will voluntarily work in union with each other for the common good. History reveals that political unions were a result of centralization via political force and military might rather than voluntary consent. Christianity provided the basis of a community united, not by external bonds, but by the vital force of distinctive ideas and principles emanating from internal decisions.

In the Bible's history the term "covenant" expressed this idea of social frameworks of government, especially in early Israel. As Christianity emerged and influenced different nations, these governing principles spread and civil agreements or contracts became a part of other nations. In early America, English Pilgrims drafted the Mayflower Compact in 1620 for their civil government which stated their agreement to covenant together to create a system of congregational church government. The modern concept of constitutionalism is based upon this Biblical idea of covenant [Study this further in the third book in this series on 'Taking Up Serpents']. Many nations have adopted constitutions in the last few centuries but have lacked the biblical foundation and the individual character that was, for thousands of years, the basis upon which covenants were founded.

Covenants are a foundational part of a nation. The Bible contains covenants between man and man and between God and man. The ultimate covenant (Matt 26:28) that God makes with men through the atoning work of Jesus Christ initiates the heart change that is necessary for the foundation of freedom in an individual and in a nation. Biblical marriage covenants keep marriages permanent and strong. Without strong families, no nation can long endure.

The external union of a people in covenants develops from an internal unity of ideas and principles residing in the hearts of the people.

Compulsory unions, imposed by external force and fear, never last. Even when a nation tries to establish an external written form of government in a constitution, it rarely succeeds due to a military coup soon thereafter. For instance, Venezuela has had 26 constitutions since its independence about two centuries ago. Haiti has had 24.

A framework of government (or union) cannot be forced externally, but must arise from internal agreement. Covenants or compacts among people on a local level are the basis of political unions. For people to covenant together, they must share common beliefs, purposes, ideas, and faith. Joining together for civil purposes in our nations begins with covenanting together for independent purposes in homes, churches, schools, clubs, businesses and various organizations. A people together in harmonious union will bring a great increase to the strength of a country.

The principles of self-government and union must be balanced. Too much emphasis on political union will result in centralization of power, while too much emphasis on self-government leads to disintegration of the nation.

Pray for more voluntary union and working together by covenant in your nation's people and leaders. Prophetically proclaim for it to emerge.

3. Individuality/Diversity

The principle is simply that everyone created by God is unique and distinct. Everyone has a well-defined existence with unique talents and abilities designed for a special purpose. Mankind has physical characteristics that make us distinct from other people - fingerprints, profile, voiceprints, scent, and even nerve patterns on the inside of the eye. We have matchless internal characteristics including thoughts, opinions, emotions, and attitudes.

Man is a reflection of his Creator, who is unified (God is One), yet diverse (God is a triune Being). God does not create carbon-copy molds of humans, animals, trees, minerals, mountains, rivers, planets or stars. Everything He creates is unique. Every person has his own outward and inward identity or individuality (Note: God's creation is perfect and should be respected, but man can wrongly use the concept of "individuality" to claim that everyone must respect them although they make choices that are in violation of God's design, such as homosexuality and transgender debates today). Each is responsible and accountable for his/her own choices and actions.

While the principle of individuality clearly reflects that all men are equal in their right to life, liberty, and the pursuit of acquiring property, men are not equal in their talents and abilities. Governments embodying false ideas of equality say that men have an equal right to material possessions and then try to distribute the wealth accordingly. Equal opportunities from God are different from the equal outcomes attempted by men. All men have equal rights before the law and governments exist to secure those rights.

We must be careful to keep a balance of individual diversity with covenantal unity as discussed earlier. Too much emphasis on individual diversity leads to anarchy and unchecked and dangerous elements. This was evident in ancient democracy of Greece where liberty was abused and led to chaos and eventually the rise of a new dictator. In modern America and other western cultures today we see that it is abused and special advantages are claimed in the name of individuality, especially sexual and gender identity, and this is now producing a fascist repression of different opinions.

Conversely, the result of an over-emphasis on unity is tyranny. This exaltation of the group over the individual is seen in many Asian cultures and often supports a totalitarian style of government such as seen in late 20th century Soviet Union or the Chinese Communism of Mao. The proper balance of unity and diversity, embodied in a decentralized, democratic constitutional republic, will produce liberty while also maintaining order in a society. Man, being created by God, has an independent value. In a nation that views the state as paramount in value rather than the individual, the people's lives, liberty, and property will always be in danger.

Pray for more individuality and respect for diversity in your nation's people and leaders. Prophetically proclaim for it to emerge.

4. Property

A person's property is whatever he has the exclusive right to possess and control. The most precious property is one's conscience which tells a person whether his actions are right or wrong. Each person in a free nation has the responsibility to be a good steward of his conscience and keep it clear. By doing so, he will know what is right and wrong from within and therefore will be able to live his life in a right manner. The apostle Paul said he did his "best to maintain always a blameless conscience both before God and before men" (Acts 24:16).

How one manages his internal property determines how he takes care of his external property. The following columns list kinds of internal and external property:

Internal Property	External Property
Thoughts	Land/Estate
Opinions	Money
Talents	Freedom of Speech
Conscience	Bodily Health
Ideas	Possessions
Mind	Freedom of Assembly

The famous British political scientist, John Locke, wrote in his treatise *Of Civil Government* that while we are God's property, God has given us the responsibility to be good stewards over ourselves. He wrote that "every man has a Property in his own Person." We have a God-given right to everything necessary to preserve our persons, i.e. a right to internal and external property. God requires us to be good stewards of everything we have.

Before any property can be taken from us, we must give our consent. If our property can be taken without our consent, then we really have no property. A people standing on the principle of property will prohibit government or other citizens from seizing anyone's personal property without their consent, or from violating anyone's conscience and rights. Lack of this principle leads to unjust taxation, a government-controlled economy, and usurpation of both internal and external property rights.

Pray for a greater value of property, especially the internal kind, in your nation's people and leaders. Prophetically proclaim for it to emerge.

5. Education

An ignorant people will quickly become an enslaved people. Only a well-instructed citizenry can be permanently free. To preserve liberty in a nation, the general populace must understand the principles upon which a free government is based. When they do, they will prevent leaders from eroding their God-given rights.

Education is a sowing and reaping process. The Bible likens it to the cycle of a plant. The "seed principle" laid out in the well-known parable of the sower and the soils (Mark 4) is essential for us to understand in order to value education. The kingdom of God is like a seed. Although we are instantly converted when we repent and submit ourselves to Christ, the establishment of God's character and kingdom within us is a gradual ongoing process, like the growth of a plant. A seed is planted; nourishment, care, and sunlight are provided; pruning is done; and then a mature plant comes forth bearing fruit.

This same principle applies in establishing God's truth in the nations of the world. It is a gradual process that occurs through Christian education. The ideas that are sown in a people through education will grow over the years and produce fruit that can be seen in every aspect of life—personal, social, political, and economic. An example would be Europe, where the emergence of universities around 1100 A.D. dramatically accelerated that continent in terms of liberty and prosperity compared to other regions of the world over the next eight centuries. And the United States was even more dramatic in its rise to a world power in intellectual and economic resources, after its priority on education beginning just a few centuries earlier.

Someone once said "the philosophy of the schools in one generation will be the philosophy of government in the next." Educational institutions lay the foundation for liberty or bondage, depending upon the ideas imparted. Education is the means for propagating either a mandated governmental philosophy or a biblical self-governed way of life.

For a free government to be sustained, the people need more than knowledge or facts - they need moral and principled education. Education in the Christian religion and morality must be primary to information and knowledge because the most fundamental and universally accepted principles for free societies have their genesis in the Bible. The educational systems of pagan governments will not teach these to our children. The responsibility of maintaining a free nation rests on families, churches, and private Christian schools that will educate the next generation in morality and Christian principles.

Pray for more godly (especially private Christian) schools and valuing of knowledge in your nation's people and leaders. Prophetically proclaim for it to emerge.

6. Morality

No nation can long endure without personal virtue and morality. A loss of principles and manners is the greatest threat to a free people and will cause its downfall more surely than any foreign enemy. When the people are virtuous they cannot be subdued, but once virtue is forfeited, liberties are surrendered to the first external or internal invader.

Character is a convictional belief that creates consistent behavior. Character literally means "to stamp and engrave through pressure." God is stamping and engraving upon us His image so that we might be examples of Him to the world by fulfilling His purpose for our lives. History has shown that virtue and character in a people are the basis of happiness in a society and absolutely necessary for a state to long remain free.

People of character will desire to observe and respect the law and will not willfully take the life, liberty or property of others. In addition, less government will be required in a virtuous nation since the rulers will also more likely be moral. Virtuous leaders allow freedom and justice to flourish because they do not corrupt the system. Consequently, people will not live in fear of civil government and generally do more than what law requires.

A lack of character in the people produces the following: a stagnant or declining economy, corrupt laws, a lack of smooth transition from one political leader or party to another after elections, a corrupt military that takes control of the government, and increased power and growth in civil government. Too many character flaws in the people create a greater need for external control. People of character will be eternally vigilant to secure their rights and demand that their government's power remain limited.

Pray for more pursuit of morality and character in your nation's people and leaders. Prophetically proclaim for it to emerge.

7. Faith in God and His Word

The foundational principles and the framework of a free society originate in the faith or religion of the people. The principles come from the Bible. Man becomes self-governing and able to live these principles when he is subject to God and His truth. Morality cannot exist without religion.

For the fundamental rights of man to be secure from government, the people must recognize that these rights are endowed by the Creator and not granted by government. If government is the source of rights, then government can take away those rights. But if God gives rights to men, then they are inalienable and absolute.

The following question must be answered and understood correctly to secure liberty for all men. "Who is the source of law in a society?" The source of law in a society is the god of that society or the cult of that culture. If man is the law's final source, then the law will constantly change as man's ideas and understanding changes. God alone is the source of true law and His law is absolute. William Blackstone, the great English legal scholar, said that no human laws are of any validity, if contrary to the higher law of God.

The Bible, the written Word of God, is the primary method through which God reveals His law to man. The degree to which nations apply the principles of the Bible will be the degree to which those nations prosper and remain free. The civil liberty now enjoyed in much of the world owes its origin to the principles of the Christian religion. Genuine Christianity gave birth to free constitutions of government. This began with Israel in the Bible and its written constitution called the "book of the covenant" and emerged due to Christian influence in Europe such as Alfred's 9th century England, then the 13th century Magna Charta, and later America's Constitution in 1789. Belief in God and the Bible matters in the history of nations.

Pray not only for more people to be saved and for revival to come, but for more faith in God and respect for His Word in your nation's people and leaders.

Ekklesia Prayer and the Power for Changing a Nation

When these seven areas are developed and cultivated in a nation, liberation begins that is revolutionary and long-lasting. Many people want and pray for bad leaders in their nation to be removed. These type of revolutions may happen quickly, but without a biblical national morality, the result rarely produces lasting good.

The pathway to liberty within a nation is from the internal to the external. This is true for civil governments, churches, homes, businesses, or associations. The power, which is internal, precedes the change, which is external. The power of a free nation is revealed by its internal principles. These principles make a strong foundation, providing proper support for individuals, families, churches, associations, and governments. These pillars enable societies to withstand any pressure and develop a free, just, prosperous, peaceful, and long-lasting culture. Without this foundation, a free government can never be established or maintained.

We must focus our prayer meetings on not only standing against darkness in our country but also on praying the good in these seven areas that can bring real power for godly biblical change in a nation. This is perhaps what Jesus envisioned when He said he would build His church, but used a non-religious Greek term for it – Ekklesia (Matt 16:18). It was the word for the governing group of people in cities that gathered to solve problems. They were not religious assemblies at all, but problem-solving management bodies in local communities.

When we gather as a church, an Ekklesia of Christ, we then should pray for real solutions and make decrees in alignment with God's kingdom purposes. This is Ekklesia prayer. When we do so, the nation's demons are cast out and the Spirit of the Lord comes in their place.

Recommended Resources on City-oriented, Research-based, Unified Prayer and prophetic Proclamation

Ekklesia by Ed Silvoso
Possessing the Gates by Cindy Jacobs
Take Back the Night by Candi MacAlpine
The Journey to Transformation Curricula by George Otis Jr.
Informed Intercession by George Otis Jr.
Prayer Altars: a Strategy That is Changing Nations, John Mulinde, Mark Daniel
Can You Feel the Mountains Tremble? by Dr. Suuqiina
Releasing Heaven On Earth by Alistair Petrie
Taking Our Cities for God by John Dawson
That None Should Perish by Ed Silvoso

Chapter 2

REACH OUT: Outward-oriented Apostolic Evangelism

Ezra 9:9 **"reviving (us) to set up the house of God, to repair its ruins"**
1 Tim 2:7 **"ordained a preacher, and an apostle...of the Gentiles"**

July 1979, Lexington, Massachusetts, USA
As thirty of us looked at the old town church across the lawn known as Lexington Green, a National Park Service tour guide told the story of the midnight right of Paul Revere to the local pastor's home that night to warn the patriot leaders, Sam Adams and John Hancock, of the approaching British soldiers. The men of the church gathered at dawn on the church green under the command of Deacon Parker who had been militarily drilling them regularly as part of his deacon duties. Their pastor, Jonas Clarke, had taught them that resisting tyranny was obedience to God. He had served on the town council helping to advise and draft governmental documents and statements based on a Biblical worldview.
Suddenly during that monologue I sensed something happening to me. Not audibly, but just as real, I heard God tell me of my mission. I was a young pastor from a different Lexington in the state of Kentucky. On vacation visiting historical sites along the east coast, I had started reading a book by Peter Marshall called *The Light and the Glory*. It told of colonial pastors who God used to write documents of liberty, found renowned universities of Harvard, Yale, and Princeton, and serve in development of diverse community institutions of medicine, media, business, and more.

Up to that point, I had been faithful to do as I learned in bible school and pastoral training, to preach God's word, counsel the flock, evangelize the community, and pray for revival just as every other minister I knew. But God was speaking to me in that moment on the Lexington Green to study and learn scriptural truths about nations in order to mentor leaders as the colonial pastors did during that important time in history. I sensed God telling me to prepare myself for Him to use me to equip pastors to not just grow their church but disciple their nation.

I would look back afterwards and recognize it as the moment that God delivered an apostolic appointment to me. Three dozen years later, the fulfillment of the Lord's words to me that day on Lexington Green can be clearly seen. I taught my congregation of God's mission for them beyond the walls of the church and prepared them to impact their city and nation. Other pastors began to recognize the influence within our city and asked for help. The discipleship materials turned into books and seminars, a Biblical Worldview University, and a Global Transformation Network that currently serves leaders in over 40 countries. My church was never very big in numbers, but certainly big in impact, being felt in Charlottesville, Virginia, America, and the world.

The Great Commission of Jesus Christ found at the end of the Gospels, was given just before His ascension. It states that Christ's followers are to go and "preach" to every individual (Mark 16, anthropos), and to "disciple all the nations" (Matthew 28:19,20, ethnos). Some English translations fail to show the word "disciple" here as a Greek verb in the imperative mood (i.e. a commandment). They thus sometimes say "make disciples of all the nations", which sounds like a personal activity *within* a nation rather than a corporate activity *to* a nation. Very different.

The passage shows that this mission was to be done in three ways: "go(ing)", "baptizing' and "teaching". These verbs are present participles that describe how the imperative verb is to be carried out. Of the 15 times Jesus uses the word baptize (i.e. "immerse"), only 3 referred to water (other baptisms in suffering, Holy Spirit, etc), so here it means go and saturate the nations in God's name.

Most pastors today focus on growing the number of individual Christians, increasing the size of their programs and buildings, and caring for those that are gathered there. These are worthy aims, but transforming the nations that God created ought to be the proper end goal. It is likened unto the focus of a coach being to recruit players onto their team, get them in shape, and understanding the playbook, and thinking that in itself is success! But no team is a success until it gets into the game, scores the goals and wins the championship. The church is the team. The building is the locker room. But the game is the nation. We must go out, push back darkness, in every sphere of society, and transform the nation.

When we look at the life of the Apostle Paul and his journey to Athens, we see that he didn't go to the synagogue as we might expect. Instead, he went to the open marketplace of ideas. It was there that he articulated God's perspective on nations found in Acts 17:24-28:

The God who made the world and all things in it since he is Lord of heaven and earth does not dwell in temples made with hands; neither is He served by human hands, as though He needed anything, since He Himself gives to all life and breath and all things; and He made from one, every nation of mankind to live on all the face of the earth, having determined their appointed times, and the boundaries of their habitation that they should seek God, if perhaps they might grope for Him and find Him, though He is not far from each one of us; for in Him we live and move and exist.

God is not only sovereign in the historical development of nations — He made every nation and determined when they would exist – but he has also determined their boundaries. Each continent and nation have a unique destiny or purpose, as well as a unique geographic, ethnic and cultural structure. A biblical apostolic vision for revival and awakening is much bigger than just a church, it must include the nation.

Providential History and Purpose of Every Nation

As Paul proclaimed, not just Israel, but every nation has been created by God for a unique purpose. French Historian Charles Rollin expressed the view of many eighteenth-century writers that God is sovereign over history and deals with nations according to the hearts and actions of the people. He wrote:

> Nothing gives history a greater superiority to many branches of literature, than to see in a manner imprinted, in almost every page of it, the precious footsteps and shining proofs of this great truth, viz. that God disposes all events as Supreme Lord and Sovereign; that He alone determines the fate of kings and the duration of empires; and that he transfers the government of kingdoms from one nation to another because of the unrighteous dealings and wickedness committed therein.

Divine Providence shapes the history of nations. George Bancroft, eminent historian of American history in the 19th century said, "Providence is the light of history and the soul of the world. God is in history and all history has a unity because God is in it." Providential history is true history. Many modern educators deny the Providential view of history. They would lead us to believe that secular views of history are simply the honest recounting of the "facts" while failing to acknowledge the pagan, humanistic presuppositions that determine their retelling of the "facts" and determine which people, places, principles, and events they deem important. Such scholars fail to communicate the fundamental truth that neutrality is not possible when teaching history. A historian's worldview will always dictate his perspective of history.

Just as there may be differing interpretations of Scripture (2 Pet. 1:20, 21), the same is true for history. Ultimately though there is only one correct view, that of the Author's. And history is His-Story, the autobiography of Him '*who worketh all things after the counsel of His will*' (Eph. 1:11) and Who is graciously timing all events after the counsel of His Christ, and the Kingdom of God on earth. The Bible overwhelmingly affirms this truth.

1 Timothy 6:15 — *"He is the blessed and only Sovereign, the King of Kings and Lord of lords."*

Proverbs 16:9-10—*"The mind of man plans his way, but the Lord directs his steps. A divine decision is in the lips of the king."*

Job 12:23—*"He makes the nations great, then destroys them; He enlarges the nations, then leads them away."*

Psalms 22:28—*"For the kingdom is the Lord's, and He rules over the nations."*

Daniel 2:21—*"It is He who changes the times and the epochs; He removes kings and establishes kings."*

Daniel 4:17, 26—*"The Most High is ruler over the realm of mankind;... Your kingdom will be assured to you after you recognize it is Heaven that rules."*

Acknowledging the Providence of God in history is the foundation for transforming the seven areas of culture. Each nation should study to see the hand of God in their country and to know their own Providential history. If we do not recognize the hand of God in our nation, how will we be able to fulfill our God-given purposes?

Why The Influence of Christianity is Weak in a Nation

Unfortunately, many modern pastors incorrectly believe that revival, evangelism and growing congregations is all that is needed to change a nation. In contrast, an early American pastor, Dr. Jedidiah Morse, preached an insightful election sermon in 1799 from the Biblical text: "If the foundations be destroyed, what can the righteous do?" (Psalm 11:3). In it, he said: "To the kindly influence of Christianity we owe that degree of civil freedom, and political and social happiness which mankind now enjoys. In proportion as the genuine effects of Christianity are diminished in any nation, either through **unbelief** or the **corruption of its doctrine**, or the **neglect of its institutions**; in the same proportion will the people of that nation recede from the blessings of genuine freedom, and approximate the miseries of complete despotism...."

A nation becomes weak first because of **unbelief**. A majority of the population does not need to be converted for a country to become or remain a godly nation. Rarely in history has a nation possessed a majority of genuine believers. A committed minority that understands responsibility, leadership and influence can shape a nation. Unbelief is counteracted in a nation when preaching, major revival and spiritual awakenings occur. This creates a strong core of the population that follows Christ and his teaching.

A nation cannot be blessed without strong vibrant churches led by dedicated godly preachers. But according to Ephesians 4:11-12 the evangelist is to equip the rest of the church members to work "the fields that are white to harvest." The church will never be effective if it has determined that only a few evangelize or invite people to church. The church grows when everyone recognizes his/her responsibility to interact with a lost and dying world.

A missional approach rather than an attractional model is key to growing the numbers of believers in a nation. Much of modern western European and American styles of evangelism are based on the attractional model which is mainly based on trying to bring people to a church. This strategy works somewhat when there is an overwhelming Christian culture and large numbers of believers. In contrast, a missional model takes the church out to where people are, seeking to meet needs there and finding a way to relate the gospel to people who have no inclination to ever attend a church. This is what Christians do today around the world in Islamic or other cultures that do not allow churches to operate openly anyway.

We can see the effectiveness of a missional approach in the growth of the early church.

The missional impact of the early church

In the history of nations the growth of Christianity has been phenomenal. Unbelief has never been a match for biblically authentic Christianity. When we look at the early church, we can see the impact of a missional approach to transform nations. Christians were actively going out to unbelievers in every neighborhood and sphere of culture. The result was a spiritual awakening for many nations. In the first three centuries after Christ's ascension, there were no church buildings. The church was primarily missional, meeting wherever the people were - homes, businesses, public meeting places, etc. As seen below, they slowly transformed the Roman Empire both by evangelism and confronting pagan ideologies in the culture:

- 65, The entire Roman Empire heard the gospel says Clement of Rome
- 66, Thaddeus goes to Armenia; Thomas is martyred in India (72AD)
- C. 100, First Christians in Sri Lanka and Algeria
- 174, First Christians in Austria
- 180, Pantaenus preaches in India
- 180s, Irenaeus in France documents prophecies, tongues, exorcisms, healings, visions, resurrections occurring in evangelism.
- 196, Christians in the Persian empire (Iran)

- 200, First Christians in Switzerland and Belgium
- 208, First Christians in Scotland
- 250, Denis is first missionary in Paris, France
- C. 250, In Turkey Gregory the Miracle Worker sees signs and wonders
- C. 270, Anthony and Pachomius start monasticism in Egypt where healings, exorcisms, miracles, signs and wonders are documented
- 295, Dudi of Basra preaches in India
- 300, First Christians in central Asia and Afghanistan
- c. 340s, Goths in Romania evangelized by Ulfilas (non-Trinitarian)
- 354, Christians reported in India
- 354, Christians now living on Socotra islands south of Yemen
- 364, conversion of Vandals

There had always been persecution in this era but especially 284-305, when Diocletian the Roman emperor, persecuted and killed about a million Christians. Truly, despite great opposition, after just three centuries the number of Christians expanded from 12 disciples to 12% of the world's population despite losing over a million Christians to martyrdom! An evangelistic witness had reached nearly 40% of the world's population with Christians and churches not only in Europe and north Africa but as far east as Afghanistan, India, and Sri Lanka and south to Ethiopia. It was starting to reach nations outside of the Roman Empire. The scriptures had been translated into 10 languages. Nearly 50% of the Roman Empire had converted to Christianity.

But purely evangelism was not the whole story. They confronted the pagan culture with God's standards of life. In 363, the last pagan emperor Julian said of Christians as he lay dying: "You have conquered." Christians cared the poor and began to change ideas about slavery, marriage, sexuality, abortion and more. Here are some examples in this same time period of cultural transformation activity:

- C. 100 Ovidius of Gaul emancipates 5000 slaves. Hermes, a Roman prefect, emancipates 1200.
- 126 Galen, a Greek pagan, says Christians are known for "self-control" & "pursuit of justice".
- C. 150 Justin Martyr says that collections are taken regularly during church to help orphans and to start schools in Ephesus (Turkey) and Rome (Italy). He condemns prostitution and "sodomy" and promotes marriage "so that we may bring up children."
- 168, Theophilus of Antioch condemns "incest and sodomy."
- 180, Clement of Alexandria founds the School of Alexandria (Egypt) and condemned sexual immorality and taking drugs to cause abortion.
- C. 200 Tertullian condemned child-abandonment and abortion and admonished Christians to not attend gladiator contests. He said that churches had a common fund to which they gave voluntarily for the support of widows, disabled, orphans, sick, prisoners, teachers, burials for the poor, money to buy slaves their freedom, etc.
- 220, Tertullian says since homosexuality is: "beyond the laws of nature, we banish...from all shelter of the Church, because they are not sins, but monstrosities." "The Christian [man] confines himself to the female sex....[and] has nothing to do with any but his own wife."
- C. 300, Bishop Methodius: "the sin of Sodom is contrary to nature....All these things are forbidden...'Thou shalt not lie with mankind as with womankind. For such a one is accursed, and ye shall stone them with stones: they have wrought abomination.'"
- 319, Eusebius of Caesarea: "[H]aving forbidden...the union of women with women and men with men, he [God] adds: `Do not defile yourselves with any of these things' [Lev. 18:24-25]."
- 321 Christians start first mental asylums and first orphanages.
- 320 In resistance to Licinius the eastern emperor, several bishops and forty Roman soldiers refused to renounce their faith and died.
- 325 Council of Nicaea instructed all churches in major cities to start a hospice to provide medical care plus shelter for the poor.
- 360, Martin of Tours establishes the west's first monastery in Poiters (2nd in Tours, 372). Promoted scholarship and learning.
- 363, The last pagan emperor Julian complained that only Christians "relieve both their own poor and ours."

The previous list of activities above shows the comprehensive approach that early Christians applied to reach the dominant pagan culture - healing, giving to the poor, teaching and modeling Biblical sexuality and ethics, resisting tyranny, etc. These Christians did not adopt the popular notion that remaining quiet about controversial issues would make Christians more likable and the church larger. Instead, they did not shy away from taking moral stands contrary to the culture on issues like abortion, prostitution, etc. They were not just having religious meetings and hoping that unbelievers would attend. They did not have a narrow goal of only gathering for worship and "winning souls for heaven." In fact, not a single church building had been erected for worship! Through their missional model of ministry, they "conquered" evil with good (Rom 12:21). The culture of Europe and the Middle East was being transformed and now even those at the top began to convert or at least require toleration of Christianity:

- 301, Gregory the Illuminator converts King Tiridates I of Armenia.
- 311, Eastern Roman Emperor Galerius issues *Edict of Toleration*, ending persecution in the eastern Empire.
- 312, Conversion of Western Emperor Constantine the Great. In 313 his *Edict of Milan* officially declared religious freedom.
- 326, King Mirian III (Miraeus) of Georgia converts to Christianity due to female Turkish evangelist named Nina
- 328, Frumentius preaches in Ethiopia where King Ezana of Axum is Christian (1st ruler outside Roman empire to convert).

Truly, they were now seeing incredible cultural transformation at every level of society. The Great

Commission was being fulfilled. This entire transformation of nations occurred without direct state-favored status. Motivation for transformation came from active Christian citizens informing and influencing the adoption of policies and laws for the good of all.

The missional impact of the church in the early Middle Ages (c350-c650AD)

Meanwhile, other nations outside the Roman Empire began to be evangelized. Evangelistic history of the church in this period abounds with stories of how Christians dramatically won people to Christ with powerful preaching, spiritual gifts and miracles, and practical service. Over the next three centuries the great Fathers of the Church (and occasional women such as Brigid) emerged within the Empire to not only organize religious activities but also using greater civil freedom to establish transformational institutions to solve cultural problems. See below examples of both evangelism and community transformation (note that memtion of "monasteries" signifies promotion of academic transformation and scholarship):

- C. 350, Basil of Caesarea and Chrysostom of Constantinople started orphanages. Gregory of Nazianzus worked for laws on adultery to apply to men same as women. Christians helped reform prisons to protect women by separating them from men for first time.
- 369, Basil starts 1st hospital [xenodochium] in history [Cappadocia]; 2nd in Edessa, 375. Both miracles and medicine used to reach the lost.

- 386, Jerome founded Bethlehem monastery; Documents numerous healings & exorcisms in evangelism; Condemned practice of drug-induced abortion. In 404 he writes Latin Bible for Europeans.
- 390, Bishop Ambrose of Milan documents healings & tongues in evangelism. In 397 Ambrose defends rights of Jewish clergy.
- 390, Nestorian missionary Abdyeshu builds monastery in Bahrain.
- 395, Augustine of Hippo becomes bishop; In 426 he writes *City of God* with providential world history. In it and *The Retractions* he rejects his earlier belief that miracles had ceased and documents evangelistic miracles, exorcisms, healings, visions, and resurrections.
- c. 397, Ninian converts Picts; founded monastery in Galloway, Scotland.
- 398, John Chrysostom of Constantinople; starts hospitals & charities
- C. 400, Schools in liberal arts begin at cathedrals; open to unbelievers.
- C. 400, Melania, a wealthy roman woman, & Chromatius, a Roman Prefect, emancipate c10,000 slaves
- 404, Martyrdom of Telemachus after protesting in Rome's colosseum against gladiator fights; causing Emperor Honorius' edict banning it in the west (as did Theodosius I in the east).
- 420, Arabian Bedouin tribe converted by sheik/bishop Peter-Aspebet
- 425, First bishops for Afghanistan and Uzbekistan
- 428, Nestorius becomes patriarch of Constantinople.
- 432, Patrick goes to Celtic Ireland and later writes of evangelistic visions, tongues, healings, miracles, exorcisms. 445 founded Armagh monastery & schools that become best in Europe.
- C. 440, Shenouda the Great, leader of independent Coptic Church in Egypt.
- 445, Bishop Leo I persuades Attila & Huns to not sack city of Rome.
- C. 450, monastery/nunnery schools begin and include girls.
- 451, Fourth church council at Chalcedon condemns supremacy of the state (statism)
- 476, Brigid is given the nun's veil by Mel in Celtic church, Ireland. She later (490) founds a double monastery at Kildare; is abbess and later ordained as the first woman bishop in church history.
- 484, Founding of Assyrian/Nestorian monastery by Sabbas (& academy in Edessa).
- 496, Bishop Remigius of Rheims convinced the Frankish chieftain, Chlodwech (Clovis) to switch from Arian to Trinitarian Catholic faith.
- 500, first Christians in north Yemen
- 529, Justinian the Great, Byzantine emperor, abolished all laws that prevented freeing of slaves and issues *Corpus Juris Civilis* which is a Christianization of Roman law. Starts building Hagia Sophia, Instanbul.
- 528, Benedict of Nursia founds Monte Cassino monastery in Italy and also a scriptoria to copy and preserve manuscripts.
- 535, Nestorian missionaries go eastward along the silk road.
- 541, Jacob Baradeus organizes Church in western Syria (Jacobites).

- 542, Julian & Theodore evangelize Nubia (today's southern Egypt and northern Sudan). Longinus evangelizes in Sudan in 569.
- 560, Comgall founds monastery at Bangor, Ireland with 4000 students chanting praises 24 hours a day (1/3 asleep at all times). Ceaseless praise lasted almost 300 years until the Danes invaded.
- 550, St. David converts Wales to Christianity
- 563, Columba of Ireland goes to Iona, Scotland; establishes monastery that becomes best of Britain and burial place of kings & monks.
- 578, Conversion of An-numan III, last of Lachemids Arab princes.
- 580, Gregory of Tours reports miracles, healings, exorcisms in France.
- 587, Visigoths of Spain converted to Christianity
- 589, Lombards of Italy converted to Christianity
- 590, After plague killed about half of Europe, Irish missionaries Columbanus, Gall and 11 others found monasteries at Luxeuil and 93 other locations in France, Switzerland, Germany, Austria, Italy and Ukraine. They rebuild Christian Europe with Celtic emphasis on ceaseless prayer, scholarship and Patrick's laws of government.
- 590-604, Gregory the Great documents miracles, visions, prophecies while serving as Pope and the de facto civil ruler of the former western Roman Empire. Sends Augustine to Britain in 597 & converted the West Saxon king, Ethelbert; baptizes ten thousand.
- 625, Paulinus of Wales goes to Northumbria, England and converts king Edwin. In 634 Aiden of Ireland founded monastery at Lindisfarne (Holy Isle), England. Bede documents healing miracles.
- 629, Amandus evangelizes the Slavs along the Danube (Slovakia).
- 635, Nestorian monks such as A-lo-pen (i.e. Abraham) arrives in Chinese capital of Xi'an (formerly Chang'an) during Tang dynasty. This "Illustrious" or "Luminous" religion was legally tolerated by Emperor Tai-tsung in 638, and a church was erected in Ch'ang-an.

The number of Christians during this period doubled from 12% of the world's population to 24% despite losing almost three million to martyrdom. About the time of the fall of the western Roman empire in 476, Christianity began to develop into independent expressions (besides Roman Catholic or Eastern Orthodox) by identifying with and transforming the pagan cultures of different countries (e.g. Celtic, Saxon, Coptic, Assyrian, Armenian, Ethiopian, Chinese). By the 7th century, 35% of the world's population had heard the Gospel due to missional activity.

But this history also provides numerous examples of scripture being manipulated for selfish gain. Over time, the church and state in the Roman Empire became unhealthily intermingled through the misguided good intentions of converted Emperors and other kings who sought to use state power to bless citizens. Their immaturity and lack of a consistent biblical worldview led to coercive and improper use of the state as a means of forced conversions. They outlawed all other religions and seized pagan temples to give them to the church instead.

In Europe the church gradually became stagnant and institutional. as Christianity began to have its own buildings and prestige in Europe and other places by the early middle ages, growth began to plateau. Conversions became more representations of political alliances rather than authentic apostolic evangelism. Corruption grew in the church including the first institutionalized persecution of Jews. This resulted eventually in a major split between the western and eastern churches in Europe leading to a formal division between Roman Catholic and Eastern Orthodox Christianity.

In 627 Byzantine Emperor Heraclius defeated Sassanid Persians and in 629 recovered Jerusalem but the church was so divided and weak in the Middle

East, it was unable to resist a new threat. Being weak, it was not new beliefs that conquered Christianity, but a new religion of Islam that used terrorism and warfare. From the middle of the 7th century onward, the story of Christianity changed significantly due to the rise of Islam. Besides destroying much of the church there and north Africa, Islam cut off easy communication with branches of Christianity to the east and south of the European continent.

For the church to grow again after this and the stagnation of church life in Europe in the 7th-13th centuries, there would have to be a return to missional ministry.

Re-emergence of missional ministry in late Middle Ages

The early church focused on Christ's exhortation to things being "proclaimed from the housetops" (Matt 10:27). For 2000 years of church history, true revivals grew out of an understanding of the apostolic mission of the church, as evidenced by open air preaching and practical service out where people are rather than relying on attracting people to church buildings. Although the church was much more institutional during the middle ages onward (especially in the Greek Orthodox and Roman Catholic traditions), there were always some in that time who returned to taking the gospel outside again.

In western Europe the Catholic church permitted public ministry by special groups that were appointed for this purpose. The Franciscan Order in the Catholic Church was founded by Francis of Assisi (1182-1226) who was known for preaching outdoors, in the market-places, from church steps, from the walls of castle courtyards. Many times the early Franciscan preachers were forced to preach in the open air in order to accommodate the large crowds because the churches were simply not big enough to hold the throngs that came to hear them. Popular preachers included Berthold of Regensberg (1220-1272), Anthiony of Padua (1195-1231), and Bernardino of Siena (1380-1444). Berthold preached in eastern Germany and central Europe and was reportedly heard by up to 100,000 people in the open-air at one time.

Another order, mentored by Diego de Acebo (d. 1207) but called the Dominicans because of Dominic (1170-1221), traveled from town to town conducting open air discussion of things relevant to the public. Some Dominican preachers like Vincent Ferrer (1350-1419) were so popular they had to preach outside the church to accommodate the crowds.

Much of the groundwork for the success of Luther and the Protestant Reformation was laid by groups that arose within the Catholic Church and questioned papal authority, often risking excommunication by doing so. One such group were the Waldenses who were started by Peter Waldo (1140-1218), a wealthy merchant in Lyons, France in the 12th century. His followers traveled by twos, preaching in the streets, and reading passages of Scripture translated into the common language.

John Wycliffe (1330-1384), "the Morningstar of the Reformation" was the first to translate the Bible into the English language (from the Vulgate), and his followers gained such a reputation of traveling throughout England preaching in the streets and marketplaces, that they earned the nickname of the Lollards (i.e. babblers). In Bohemia (today Czechia), Jan Hus (1369-1415) preached in like manner, and his followers, the Hussites or Czech Brethren, grew into a strong movement that radically transformed their culture, even produced several kings in that region.

Protestant missional ministry and Missions, 1500-today

The early Protestant reformers were entirely outdoor preachers due to the fact that the church buildings were controlled by the Catholic church. It was said of William Farel (1489-1565), the pioneer of Protestantism in Western Switzerland, that he preached in every stump and stone was turned into his pulpit while every house, every street, and market-place into a church. The Protestant movement, forced to become more missional instead of attractional in its ministry, helped Christianity to begin growing again.

The Presbyterian Church was founded in Scotland by John Knox (1513-1572), first a bodyguard for a street preacher named George Wishart (1513-1536). Wishart was not allowed to preach in the churches and so preached in the market-places and fields. Later, when the Church of England was established in Scotland, Protestant preachers were banned from their pulpits and became field preachers like Richard Cameron (1648-1680) and Donald Cargill (1619-1681), proclaiming their message in the open air.

Other great apostolic movements emerged after the Reformation. The Moravians of what is today eastern Germany and Czechia started missions in many nations. Beginning with the 1730 mission to St. Thomas, the missionaries also reached Greenland (1732), Suriname (1735), Georgia (1735), South Africa (1736), Gold Coast (1736), Switzerland (1740), New York (1740), England (1740), Connecticut (1742), South Africa (1742), Wales (1743), Maryland (1745), North Carolina (1753), Jamaica (1754), India (1760), and that's not all—countless other scouting trips and short term ministries were going on all the time in many other places.

The Methodist Church, co-founded by George Whitefield (1714-1770) and John Wesley (1703-1791) is an example. Whitefield and Wesley were Anglicans, but were banned from speaking in churches. Since they were not "licensed," they took to open-air ministry, boldly proclaiming the Word to large crowds in streets and markets. Whitefield spoke to estimated crowds of 20,000 people in the open air. Both traveled throughout England and the American colonies and were instrumental in the Great Awakening, a mighty revival that swept the colonies in the eighteenth century.

Another great Methodist preacher during the Welsh Revival in Wales was Gideon Ouseley (1762-1839). He traveled on horseback and preached several times a day, without ever dismounting, in streets, fairs, and markets throughout Ireland. The Methodists were also instrumental in America's second Great Awakening which was typified by outdoor Camp Meetings where prominent pastors preached like James McGready (1763-1817), Peter Cartwright (1785-1872) and Lorenzo Dow (1777-1834)

The first Protestant missionary society was started by William Carey (1761-1834), the first missionary to India. Carey went to India and started his ministry not by building church buildings but by preaching to large crowds that gathered in the streets of the brothel district. One of his converts was a young British sailor named Robert Flockhart (1778-1857), who went back to the British Isles and preached in the streets of Edinburgh for 43 years until his death. One of Carey's associates, John

Chamberlain (1777-1821) would go to the Ganges river where Hindus gathered and commence arguing with one of the Brahmins. When the argument drew a crowd, he would preach to the assembled Hindus. Countless other famous preachers began their ministries by preaching in the streets. Charles Spurgeon (1834-1892) began preaching in the streets of London at the age of 16, continuing until he became pastor of the Metropolitan Tabernacle at age 19. Dwight L. Moody (1837-1899), a well- known preacher in Chicago and founder of the Moody Bible Institute, made a regular practice of exhorting the passersby in the evenings from the steps of the court house. The Salvation Army began with street ministry and practical care for the needy.

In the 20th century the Pentecostal and Charismatic movement emerged which now accounts for most of the growth of modern Christianity around the world. In many ways, it has been due to the fact, once again, that it was forced to operate outside of traditional settings and ministered to people in the streets.

Conclusion

Despite the new spiritual life and power of the last century, the sad reality is that church growth has again leveled off. The percentage of Christians in the world is no higher today than it was about 1900. One reason for this is the same old problem of institutional and attractional model of Christianity that has once again become dominant in Europe where numbers have dramatically declined and America where it has just recently started to decrease.

Thankfully, missionaries and indigenous churches in the global south, in Asia and other places around the world have been more missional as well as apostolic by going outside the doors of their church buildings and gathering new people that are not already Christians. Nowhere is this more evident than in China which now has more Christians than any other country, without the freedom of having church in the open. There and in other countries, Christians take the initiative to go to the people instead of trying to attract people to a church building. This was the apostolic model that changes the world.

The work of William Carey, John Wesley, and so many others in not only evangelizing but meet practical social needs, has been the key to success. There is not enough space here to speak of all of that, but suffice it say, that missional evangelism and practical service in society go hand in hand with really pushing back darkness in a nation. To cast out the demons of a nation, takes prayer, but then actually putting light in every neighborhood, street, and activity of culture. When the light is there, the darkness must retreat.

There is a need for the ministry of the apostle and evangelist as listed in Ephesians 4:11-12. There are many new books about these offices in the church today, especially the role of the apostle. More than others, the office of the apostle focuses outwardly on the community and nation, rather than inwardly on the church regulars. We commend further study on these offices to the reader. When all the offices are operating in the church or together in a community, county, or state the church becomes the positive transformational force for a nation.

Resources on Apostolic outward-oriented and service-oriented strategic Evangelism and wholistic Revival

Prayer Evangelism by Dr Ed Silvoso
Evangelism Explosion by D. James Kennedy
Somebody Cares by Doug Stringer
Exponential Culture: Believer Transformation, Disciple Multiplication by Michael L. Wilson
Renovation of the Heart in Daily Practice by Dallas Willard, Jan Johnson
Crossing Rivers, Taking Cities by Frank Damazio
Recovering Our Mission by Darrow Miller
How Christianity Changed the World by Alvin Schmidt

Chapter 3

SEND OUT: Pastoral Ministry that equips for community leadership

Jer 3:15 **"I will give you shepherds...who will feed you with knowledge and understanding"**

Eph 4:11-12 **"He gave apostles, prophets, evangelists, shepherds and teachers, to equip the saints for the work"**

2015, Hyderabad, India

Leaders gathered on the highly respected Osmania University campus for my seminar titled "Recapturing Values and Challenges for Leadership of Transformation." I spoke about many of the principles discussed in this book series. I told those gathered in this majority Hindu nation the same thing I said a few years earlier in Indonesia. There I was asked to speak in the office of the Governor of Jakarta before a mixed audience. The Governor himself was a Muslim and eventually was elected the President of Indonesia. I explained one of the key teachings of Jesus – that government is to be a servant of the people. I explained that the Creator of all things has given principles and best practices that Christians are applying all over the world for the good of the society. A Christian man that I personally invested much time with then became the new Governor of Jakarta. How can a Christian man become such a high level leader in a majority-Muslim country? While serving others in lower governmental positions, he modeled impeccable character and outstanding principles, and people of all cultures long for uncorrupt, trustworthy leadership.

This story is the same in Kenya, Colombia, the Netherlands, and many more places. A team of top

megachurch apostles and bishops in Colombia today from many denominations have united and are guiding a comprehensive discipleship strategy to raise up better political, business and educational leaders for that nation.
Newspapers and television do not tell of these things but what happened in the early centuries of Europe is now occurring the world over. I am seeing these principles work for all nations because they are from the Creator of all, not from "east" or "west" or left or right. Liberty and prosperity have come to over a third of the world's nations due to the introduction and modeling of these principles. Leaders are emerging worldwide from the Christian community with a vision for not just building a church, but blessing a nation. Discipling nations does not remove the unique good things of culture; it restores what the Creator intended all along. Thank you, God for allowing me to see and hear firsthand of the amazing transformation that is happening all over the world.

People in every culture need to know that God cares for each nation and wants to use His people to transform culture for His glory. In the previous chapter we looked at the first reason Christianity may have little influence in a nation – Unbelief. We also talked about how Apostolic Evangelism and Spiritual Revival can overcome this problem. We compared many of the evangelists and ministries of the 20th century to the early apostolic church fathers and others in history. We noted that the apostolic missional model tends to create the greatest effectiveness in evangelism.

The ministry of the apostle and evangelist is listed in Ephesians 4:11-12. But also in that passage is listed "pastors and teachers." Their role in a church is not to do all the work, but rather to equip believers to discover and fulfill their ministries. Pastors have to embrace the outward community focus of the apostle in their discipleship program so as to help every member in the congregation to become the positive transformational force in their community. There was no divide between the secular and sacred in the discipleship of the apostolic and early church. But a lack of comprehensive discipleship in the last two centuries for all areas of culture has brought limits to the blessings that God wants for many nations.

One needs only to look at Africa where today over half of the population is converted in many nations, yet tyranny, poverty, corruption, and lack of education are unchanged. There are some refreshing contrasts such as South Korea where the missionaries who went there did not have a narrow religious sense of their mission and thus the nation has been dramatically transformed in little over a century. Evangelism and church growth were the focus of the missionaries in Africa and they succeeded in that. But the whole mission of not only evangelism but also discipling leaders for the nation was the focus of the Korean missionaries. There today, yes are big churches, but also good government, honest and prosperous economies, good schools and hospitals. The contrast is between them is stunning.

Besides lack of people being converted in a nation, there are two other key reasons mentioned in a historic sermon in the previous chapter that explains why Christianity may be weak in a nation:

(2) corruption of its doctrines, and (3) neglect of its institutions. Here, in addition to apostles, true biblical pastors and teachers are essential.

Corruption of Doctrine

Corrupted doctrine in this context has nothing to do with the essential fundamentals of a typical "statement of faith" such as the Godhead, salvation, etc. The doctrines we will discuss deal instead with God's authority on the earth, which Paul articulated in Acts 17:24-27:

> *The God who made the world and all things in it since he is Lord of heaven and earth does not dwell in temples made with hands; neither is He served by human hands, as though He needed anything, since He Himself gives to all life and breath and all things; and He made from one, every nation of mankind to live on all the face of the earth, having determined their appointed times, and the boundaries of their habitation...*

In this passage, Paul speaks of four primary doctrines that have practical implications on how we view the world.

(1) Creation — "God made the world."
Our world and all that is in it did not originate by chance. When this doctrine is not taught as

an essential part of our faith, Christians neglect the field of science. Neglect always leaves a void, filled by a competing ideology - in this case, Evolution. When biblical scientific reasoning was removed from public education, Charles Darwin's *"The Origin of Species"* (1859) began to be taught as fact instead of theory and creationism gradually became an irrelevant "religious" dogma. Today, Creation scientists are beginning to restore solid reasoning and helping Christians to articulate truth rather than religious dogma.

(2) Lordship — "He is Lord of Heaven and earth."

He is the absolute master and final authority to whom all must give allegiance. Because this doctrine has been neglected, another competing ideology has gained momentum, namely secular humanism. According to the humanists, man is the measure of all things and able to determine right and wrong for himself.

(3) Providence—"He Himself gives to all life and breath and all things; . . .for in Him we live and move and exist."

God is the source of every man's provisions and all must look to Him with thanksgiving for

His gracious generosity. The neglect and corruption of God's providence and provision has been exploited by Marxist and Socialist leaders. The socialistic ideas promulgated in Karl Marx's 1844 book will not have much influence when Christians live and preach biblical principles of economics. Also, when individual interests replace the common good of the community and there is a lack of Christian character, greed and materialism grow and wealth is accumulated instead of compassionately used to meet the needs of the poor.

(4) Sovereignty—"He made . . . every nation . . . having determined their appointed times and the boundaries of their habitation."

When God's sovereignty is not taught in schools and expressed in popular culture, the existential ideology will prevail. Existentialists believe history is meaningless and the future unpredictable. Therefore, to plan and work for goals is hopeless. Their philosophy is "Eat, drink, and be merry for tomorrow we die." It is present-oriented and hedonistic. Even Christians subconsciously adopt the existential view of history when they focus too much on heaven. Without a sense of responsibility for the past, Christians fail to adequately plan for the future, and become focused on immediate self-improvement. In the last 100 years, Christians have started seeing Satan as the sovereign of this world, and Jesus as an absentee king who is concerned exclusively with building and maintaining His church until He returns to earth. The worldview of the Protestant reformers of the 16th century was diametrically opposite to this view. They saw Jesus Christ as the ruler of the earth (1 Timothy 6:16; Hebrews 2:14) and Satan as a defeated foe (John 12:3, Colossians 2:15). The God of the Bible was seen as sovereign over men and their property. The outcomes of these two differing views are important. As one writer explains:

If you believe God rules the earth:
"1. Your commission is to subdue the earth and build godly nations through evangelism and discipleship.
"2. You see Christian culture as leavening all areas of life, replenishing the earth, and blessing all mankind.
"3. All of God's world is His, and every activity is seen as a spiritual work of God.
"4. Reformation is expected if a nation is obedient to God's word."

But if you believe Satan rules the earth:
"1. Your commission is just to concentrate on saving souls from this evil world.
"2. You see Christian culture as a counter-culture, an isolated, persecuted minority in an evil world.
"3. Church activity is primary and spiritual, while worldly pursuits are secular and to be dealt with only as a necessity.
"4. Reformation is impossible since things must get worse because Satan is in control."

Ideas have consequences, and as Christians abdicate their leadership role and deny the "crown rights of Jesus Christ," the church loses her influence.

Solution: Restoration of Apostolic Doctrine/Biblical Worldview

The answer to corruption of doctrine is restoring a Biblical Worldview by recovering the historic model of pastoral ministry in the church. The role of the pastor and teacher in the instruction and discipling of church members is vital. Many pastors today sincerely believe they are teaching the word of God and discipling their people but are neglecting the whole counsel of God. The instruction of believers is often limited to personal piety and church life and rarely includes their calling in the workplace, the marketplace, or civic life. Other areas are off limits, too often thought of as worldly, or less important than church activity. Real commitment to train, organize and mobilize church members for these things rarely happens.

The reality is that most pastors will not be directly involved in politics or any of the other "mountains" of culture simply due to their limited time and focus. Pastors should indeed influence other spheres of society, but their main task is not doing it themselves but, according to Ephesians 4:12 is to equip the saints for the work of the ministry. However, this equipping of the saints must be expanded to recover what once was the mission of the historic church to be a powerful positive force for transforming nations. Only when a church's leadership is faithfully "teaching them all that I commanded" will transformation of a nation be possible.

The illustration below shows the church as the central place where Christians are trained in a biblical worldview in order to influence every area of society.

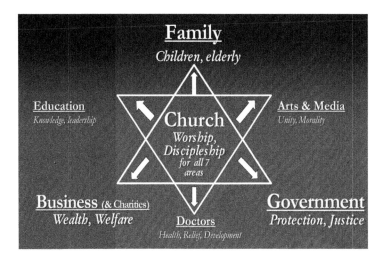

The diagram might call to mind the star of David and the nation of Israel, God's chosen nation. But today if any modern nation trains and equips the people of God to lead in all of these areas, their nation will also be blessed by God.

To become a transforming agent, a church must expand its Sunday sermons and discipleship programs beyond the exclusive focus of individual salvation, personal piety, and victory in life. Many churches include in the bible classes and small-group curriculum a focus on family. Some churches teach about work and business. But a transforming church's curriculum should include all six key areas of cultural influence: Family, Business, Education, Media, Health Care, and Government.

Throughout most of history, the clergy and church leaders deliberately discipled and trained leaders for all areas of society, and this dramatically changed nations. Nowhere is this more evident than in Colonial America where pastors used every opportunity possible to educate the people in the principles of liberty. The traditional Election Sermon, which was initiated in 1633 and occurred regularly for 250 years, was always preached before voting took place and was given to every government representative, printed in the newspapers, and studied in every home. These sermons empowered Christians with an idea of how to conduct themselves in politics and public affairs and directly contributed to prosperity and blessing in the nation. Today modern pastors do two other unhealthy extremes – they avoid talking about the election completely, or they tell their people who to vote for.

Neglect of Institutions

The third area that causes the church to become weak in any culture or nation is the neglect of the institutions that God has established and the church has historically influenced for the good of society. The seven institutions mentioned in the previous section are listed again in an order that follows the English alphabet:

Arts, Media & Entertainment
Business
Church
Doctors (i.e. Health and Science)
Education
Family
Government

Our previous survey of the early church demonstrated the multi-faceted approach the church used in its mission to disciple nations. A chronology of events after the 7th Century revealed additional examples in history where the church provided leadership for every area of life. Pastors not only taught their people, but also became examples of those leading the way in these various institutions.

Rev. John Witherspoon was a great example of an American minister in the 18th century who directly and indirectly shaped public affairs. He served as a Presbyterian pastor and President of Princeton College. Rev. Witherspoon was active in politics, a signer of the Declaration of Independence, and served on more than 100 committees in Congress during the nation's struggle for independence. His discipleship of leaders is a typical example of the colonial clergy who actively discipled their nation. While President of Princeton, Witherspoon trained not only ministers but leaders in all areas of life. One young leader came to study theology under Witherspoon, but biblical principles of law and government were so impressed upon him in his study of the Bible that he went on to become the chief architect of the United States Constitution and the fourth President of the United States — James Madison. Witherspoon also trained:

1 vice president;

3 Supreme Court justices;

10 national government executive members;

12 governors;

60 Congressmen

Plus many members of state or regional governments.

A French political philosopher, Alexis de Tocqueville, came to the United States of America in the 1830's in search of reasons why America quickly rose to power and prosperity. After a thorough examination he concluded:

"On my arrival in the United States the religious aspect of the country was the first thing that struck my attention; and the longer I stayed there, the more I perceived the great political consequences resulting from this new state of things....The Americans combine the notions of Christianity and of liberty so intimately in their minds that it is impossible to make them conceive the one without the other."

De Tocqueville declared that pastors had effectively discipled the American citizen for every area of life. There was no divide between the secular and the sacred. The church purposefully and deliberately educated the congregation about making a difference in culture. They taught and developed their people in the seven key institutions and then commissioned them to lead. Today's church must be serious about discipleship in these seven areas. When institutions are neglected, corruption and ungodliness fill the void. The result of the church in America's recent neglect of these institutions is evident today in the promotion of gay marriage, abortion, and immorality.

Solution: Restoration of Apostolic Strategy for Reformation of Society

If the church's voice is silent in the educational, economic, social, and political institutions, then people who lack Christian character and thinking will assume control of these areas. If Christians are leaders only inside the church and allow people with pagan worldviews and ungodly character to lead the other six key areas of cultural influence (i.e. the "mountains"), then Christianity will have limited impact on the culture. Consequentially when these institutions operate from a worldly philosophy, liberty and justice for all is diminished. God's best is missing. As Christians commit themselves to be "salt of the earth," corruption will subside, "the righteous will be in authority," and "the people will rejoice" (Proverbs 29:2). As it says in Proverbs 14:34, "Righteousness exalts a nation."

Pastors should adopt the proven pattern of cultural discipleship for their members that has been shown from church history. Churches can provide weekly classes for teens and adults, home-groups, or special study groups which train their members in Biblical principles for the different areas of society. Specific sermons can be scheduled to coincide with national holidays, election time, and local community events. These sermons can be preached on Sundays and at special seminars for the general community. Distributing these sermons in printed form and online also can help disseminate the truth. In addition, the church can supplement the schooling efforts of parents by starting private schools and coordinating special tutoring and events for home-schooling parents in order to help educate the next generation in a biblical worldview. Clergy can seek to develop relationships with community leaders in the government, business, and media spheres, providing biblical consultation and advice.

The pastor does not have to lead in all the seven spheres or mountains of influence but he should identify and appoint mentors in his church who can assume congregational responsibility for training in these areas. These mentors must have an apostolic mentality, organizing members to develop and fulfill strategic plans in their areas of influence beyond the church's own religious programs. A director in the church who is commissioned to lead and be accountable to the lead pastor and elders of the church, should oversee growth and discipleship in these following areas:

Individuals

Once an individual's heart has been made new by the power of the Gospel, God puts emphasis on personal duties and responsibilities. Jesus called them the greatest commandments:

1. Worship – "Love the Lord your God." (Luke 10:27, Deut. 6:5)
2. Charity – "Love your neighbor." (Luke 10:27, Lev. 19:9-18, Mt.25:35-36)

God expected man to worship Him from the beginning at creation. Love and respect of one's neighbor was part of the human mission before any church taught it or society required it. A third responsibility was to love ourselves as the basis of loving our neighbor. This love of self is not selfishness but a biblical reminder that we are not our own; we are the temple of God needing self-protection and provision. This is accomplished by work and discipline.

Family

In addition to individual and church responsibilities, Christians are expected to live in accordance with God's will in their families. Everyone is part of a family by birth and most will begin their own family. A family is simply a man, woman, and children who are related by marriage, blood, or adoption. The Creator's design for marriage is a man and woman who covenant together to fulfill God's desire for them to be fruitful and bless the world (Gen. 1:18, 22-24; 3:16). Each family's duties, according to the Bible, are as follows:

1. Procreation of children (Gen. 1:28, 1 Tim. 5:10,14) "Be fruitful and multiply"
2. Education of children (Dt. 6:6-7) "You shall teach your sons."
3. Health and Welfare, "Practice hospitality (Rom. 12:13), especially for those of your own household" (1 Tim 5:4)

The Bible teaches the family is the primary provider of education both of Christian character and knowledge. Parents should establish a regular Sabbath day time for instructing their children in the Christian history of their family, church, and nation. A regular Bible-devotional time each day in addition to a reading-aloud program in great Christian literature is necessary in every family. It is the family's responsibility, not the government's, to provide for the education of their children. Parents can work in conjunction with other home-schooling parents and church leaders to coordinate tutoring or to set up Christian schools.

Media and the Arts.

The Prophets of the Bible and Christians throughout the centuries have led the way in communications. They used creative dramatic techniques to get the attention of people and to communicate truth that was relevant to common people. Working together in voluntary union to publish books and newspapers, and in social media to reflect a Biblical worldview should be a priority. Radio, television, and movies should also be recaptured by consistent service in already existing institutions. New television networks and movie production companies must create more than just "religious" programming but also programming for all areas of society such as news networks on radio and television which will provide commentaries on everyday affairs from a Christian perspective.

Schools and Colleges.

Christians should start private schools and restore the role of family in education. But beyond the needs of their own children, quality schools must be created to meet the needs of everyone, including those children of poor and non-Christian families and children of parents who cannot or will not home-school. Christians should recapture the Universities, especially those which were started by Christians, through consistent service in the sphere of education. Christians should also start new colleges and universities to teach a Biblical worldview, like Samuel's School of the Prophets (2 Kings 13:14 and 1 Samuel 19:20), Ezekiel's synagogues and Paul's two-year program in the school of Tyrannus (Acts 19:9).

Besides equipping people in this sphere, long-term plans to coordinate and connect parents and families to form organizations to work together beyond just one church must be developed. Christians need the credentials and experience respected by unbelievers. By using the existing influence of Christians in the field to open up doors, upcoming leaders will be acclimated and ready for the future.

Business, Medicine, Government.

Every citizen has three basic responsibilities in civil government. Even if their government does not officially permit these, God still commands them to work for the right to:

1. Vote for good government leaders (Deut 1:9,13; 1 Cor 6:4)
2. Support/advise good government leaders (1 Kgs 1:11-14,34; Acts 13:6-7)
3. Oppose/resist bad government leaders (1 Kgs 12:16; Lk 10:11)

For institutions such as Business, Medicine, and Government, a director should be appointed in the church for each area, accountable to the lead pastor and elders of the church. These mentors can gather those in their area of influence and organize more teaching and training, as well as facilitate the development of a long-term strategic plan to connect those together in the church in these spheres.

Finding a way to make these areas self-sustaining is essential for long term success. Funding sources must be created that institutionalizes the strategic areas and outlives the initiators of the vision.

Summary

Business as usual in the modern church will never fully transform a nation. Increasing the number of churches, developing mega-churches, and scheduling "revivals" are not enough. We must return the church to not only teaching "all that Jesus commanded" but mobilizing the church for long-term strategic action. If we are going to fulfill the apostolic mission Christ gave us to go and "make disciples of the nations," we must restore the historic model of church, the biblical model of pastoral leadership, and a biblical worldview. We must promote a vision that transcends just growing church ministries to the real focus of Christ: discipling nations again.

Resources on Pastors providing Worldview discipleship & mobilizing in coordinated cultural transformation strategy

The Enoch Treasure: When God Walks With a Friend, by Christopher Cunningham
Center Church by Tim Keller
The Wake-up Call to Radically Abandon Our Lives to God by John Mulinde
How Should We Then Live? by Francis Schaeffer
Divorce and Remarriage: The Trojan Horse within the Church by Joseph A. Webb
Til Death Do Us Part? Biblical Marriage by Joseph A Webb
Ruling in the Gates by Joseph Mattera
Transforming Your World by John Mulinde
Rebuilding Civilization on the Bible by Jay Grimstead, Eugene Clingman
Discipling Nations by Darrow Miller
Truth and Transformation by Vishal Mangalwadi
Total Truth by Nancy Pearcey
To Change the World by James Davison Hunter
His Kingdom Come: An Integrated Approach to Discipling the Nations by Jim Stier, et al

Summary

Strategic Action Plan

Teaching All That I Commanded

God warned Israel of the danger of apostasy once they entered the promised land and began to enjoy prosperity and peace there. Sure enough, just a few centuries later, a generation arose in Israel that was unfaithful to the God and traditions of their fathers. The same has been true for many once-Christian nations. Many nations that began with a strong biblical worldview and godly institutions have repeated the folly of Israel. They began to neglect the principles and practices that produced their freedom. They lost their virtue and self-government and became prey to internal evils more dangerous than any external enemies they had faced. When people lose their virtues, they will readily surrender their liberties. But when biblical morality and worldview remain strong among the citizens, they will never be enslaved.

Jesus taught that "tares" (i.e. destructive weeds that look like wheat) are sown when the church is "asleep" i.e. neglecting her role in society (Matthew 13:24 and Proverbs 24:30-34). If a nation's problems were the result of some conspiracy of powerful enemies, the solution would be beyond the reach of most of us. Fatalism, apathy, and despair would be understandable. But they would not succeed if we do not abandon our posts. Since God says the real problem is due to our neglect, then the solution is also within our grasp. If we accept our responsibility and do our duty, we have grounds for hope.

Only when we correctly identify and diagnose the true cause of a nation's problems can we start to solve them. Christians today are likely to place the blame on various conspiracies of men: the humanists, the ACLU, the big bankers, the Trilateral Commission, the New Age Movement, the World Council of Churches, the homosexuals, the feminists, the Communists, the Pope, the media, etc. When we regard such groups as the source of our problems, we ignore the real issue. In Isaiah 8, verse 12 and 13: "You are not to say, 'It is a conspiracy!', in regard to all that this people call a conspiracy. And you are not to fear what they fear or be in dread of it. It is the Lord of hosts whom you should regard as holy. And He shall be your fear, and He shall be your dread."

Many Christians today look at the state of their nations and feel hopeless. In their hopelessness, they begin to fear political parties, non-Christian groups, or tyrannical leaders more than they fear God. This attitude diminishes our vision of the truth that God is Sovereign over the earth. God sees human conspiracies and laughs at them for He knows that what He has planned will prevail. This too should be our perspective toward the evils in our nations. Israel saw hopelessness in their impending judgment, destruction, and the end of their dreams while God saw a coming Savior. Psalm two says:

> "The kings of the earth take their stand, and the rulers take counsel together against the Lord and against His Anointed: 'Let us tear their fetters apart, and cast away their cords from us!' He who sits in the heavens laughs; the Lord scoffs at them. Then He will speak to them in His anger and terrify them in His fury: 'But as for Me, I have installed My King upon Zion, My holy mountain.'....'Thou art My Son, today I have begotten Thee. Ask of Me, and I will surely give the nations as Thine inheritance...'"

This prophecy describes the first coming of Christ, His death, His resurrection, and His absolute authority to reign. Prior to His ascension, Jesus delegated this same responsibility and authority to His church saying, "All authority has been given to Me in heaven and on earth. Go therefore and make disciples of all nations."

For pastors, Jesus makes clear what should be their primary means of fulfilling the great commission—education. The main task of pastors, according to Ephesians 4:12, is to equip the saints for the work of the ministry. They are not required to personally be involved in politics, media, schools, medicine, and reconciliation, but to equip their congregation to properly do so. When a church's leadership faithfully is "teaching them all that I commanded," then transformation of a nation is possible.

Practically, a church must expand its Sunday sermons and discipleship programs beyond the exclusive focus of individual salvation, personal piety, and victory in life. Many churches include in the bible classes and small-group curriculum a focus on family. Some churches teach work and business. As the next diagram shows, church curriculum needs to include all of the other six key areas of influence in culture - Family, Business, Education, Media, Health Care, and Government.

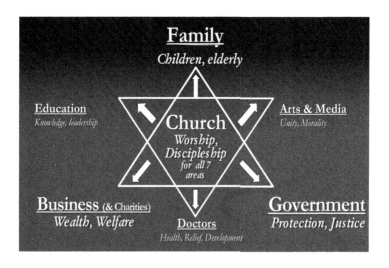

The church must train people in a biblical worldview to be able to effectively live out God's principles in each of the areas of society. This is Christ's Great Commission vision—go and disciple *all*

parts of every nation! As we do so, we can measure our progress in fulfillment of the Great Commission in the parallel passage found in Mark 16 where Jesus added "signs" that would follow this mission: casting out demons, speaking with new tongues, taking up serpents, drinking deadly things, and laying hands on the sick.

Instead of measuring our success by the size of our crowds and the size of our buildings, we should be asking ourselves, are we manifesting the "signs" Jesus mentioned in the Great Commission? Are we producing people who effectively solve spiritual, intellectual, political, economic and physical problems?

"How Nations and Cities Cast Out their Demons"

In this series of books, we look at these five signs or areas of culture needing solutions. Jesus perhaps was connecting his final message before His ascension to Moses' final message to the nation of Israel in Deuteronomy 32. There Moses warned of the problem of demons (vs 17), which was rarely mentioned in most of the Old Testament.

To cast out a nation's demons we identify three best practices or strategic actions for solving spiritual problems of sin and oppression:

- City-oriented Unified Prayer

- Apostolic outward-oriented evangelism and service
- Pastors providing Worldview Training and Mobilizing Christians in coordinated 7-sphere strategy

"How Nations and Cities Speak their New Tongues"

Another way to measure success is the degree to which its nation speaks in new tongues, not just Christians in one's prayer closet or church gathering, but in the culture. Jesus spoke these words well before Pentecost, the common reference for speaking in new tongues, and the disciples at the time were familiar with Genesis 11 where new tongues stopped Nimrod's attempt to centralize political power. The worldview of the Bible is a "new tongue" given to the church for liberating nations and empowering every demographic of society.

There are three best practices or strategic actions for solving intellectual problems of ignorance and worldview error:

- Parents and teachers providing home or church-based education of children
- Restoring Universities to Biblical Worldview and organizing other professional training in the 7 spheres

- Get Arts and Media to include biblical worldview of culture and national affairs (not just salvation)

Believers must learn to communicate truths and ideas without quoting chapter and verse, but speak to all people in a way that they can appreciate. They must journey beyond religious circles and into the culture using every means of communication possible - education, media, and the arts, etc. It includes parents schooling their kids at home, and advanced training of professionals through godly universities.

"How Nations and Cities Take Up their Serpents"

Is the church confronting and seizing the dangerous things in the culture? At the time that Jesus gave the mission of discipling nations by taking up serpents, the disciples would have associated it with the story in Exodus 3:9-10 and 4:2-4. God sent Moses to confront a powerful political leader. The Egyptian Pharoah, a tyrant, was leader of perhaps the greatest military on earth at that time. Governments of nations, both in history and modern times, often become the gathering place of "serpents." Politics is a dirty business and Christians are told by the culture to keep their distance. However, when good people stay away from government, evil and corruption fill the cultural void.

There are three best practices or strategic actions for solving political problems of injustice and tyranny:

- Putting limits on government power (through constitutions, etc) and keep it focused on protection of citizens
- Voting for good government and continuing to help good people in it
- Opposing tyranny and injustice with protest, flight and defensive force

The Bible gives a pattern of limiting the powers of the state and then exhorts that we fill its offices with good people through elections and advice, and then opposing bad officials with peaceful protest, flight and even deputized force in self-defense. It is said that "for evil men to accomplish their purpose it is only necessary that good men should do nothing." It takes the courageous efforts of righteous people to stop wicked men.

"How Nations and Cities Drink their deadly things"

Is the church confronting the deadly things in the culture? In the Song of Moses found at the end of Deuteronomy the idea of deadly drink is associated with evil in business (Deut 32:32-33). Jesus' disciples would easily have thought of this when hearing their new commission. This last criteria for measuring the church's faithfulness to the Great Commission is when corruption and ungodly practices are challenged and eliminated at the highest levels of business and finance.

There are three best practices or strategic actions for solving problems of corruption and poverty:

- Working, doing business and trade to increase wealth
- Coordinated saving of resources with others through Christian-run banks
- Coordinated giving by businesses, families and churches to care for the poor and for other community transformation goals

Biblical models of work, trade, banking and giving are different from the world and must be taught clearly. If Christians avoid personally impacting the political and business realms, that nation will never be completely transformed or fully discipled as Christ commanded.

"How Nations and Cities Lay Hands on their Sick"

A church can measure its success by the sickness not only in individuals but in culture. In 2 Chronicles 7:14 God told Israel that the land, not only individuals, would be healed if God's people acted. And who brings this healing to the land? Not governments but "people who are called by my name". To heal a nation requires that God's people "lay hands on the sick."

There are three best practices or strategic actions for solving problems of disease and divisions:

- Doctors and nurses teaching health and applying Medicine consistent with biblical worldview
- Coordinated ways to provide emergency relief for disaster victims
- Reconciling racial, tribal, religious, economic and age divisions

It takes personal engagement with those who are hurting, either through supernatural miraculous healing, or practical hands-on health care. Historically the church has been on the cutting edge of medicine, using medical missions to open nations to the gospel while opening closed hearts in the inner cities or remote areas of their own nations. The laying on of hands also means reaching across cultural and ethnic divides to heal racial divisions and other hurts caused by prejudice and disputes, some of which have simmered for centuries.

It appears from these five signs Jesus mentioned, we have insight in the heart of God for our nations and our cities. It appears He really does want us to practically look to serve and transform society. He has helped identify what a discipled nation looks like – with problems being solved the spiritual, intellectual, political, economic and physical aspects of our communities. For this to happen we must train and mobilize leaders in all seven spheres of influence in united teams and united strategy. To really succeed we need to follow the following five steps.

Five Steps to Transform Society

In the next few paragraphs we will look at practical steps that individuals and churches can take to see change in their nation. Such transformation doesn't require huge numbers or percentages of the population to be successful. One example of this is the homosexual community. Although representing just under 2% of the population of the United States, they applied a similar strategy to the one below and, in under 50 years, were able to influence the national dialogue and change the opinion of the general public and gain legal recognition of their lifestyle. With specific strategies and a concentrated effort to advance God's kingdom in the areas discussed in this book, we too can see radical transformation in our nation.

There are seven strategic resources that we must develop effectively in order to change our society:

1. new organizations working on developing new leaders in each of the 6 cultural areas such as arts, business, medicine, family, education, and politics.
2. organizations to do opposition research to expose corruption and pagan strategies
3. think tanks to provide research for strategy and winning arguments in popular cultural topics
4. social technology for networking people
5. media operations and news outlets
6. mobilization organizations for voting, protesting, and other best-practices mentioned in this book.
7. coordinated giving and funding organizations for all of the above.

The church today may be growing in numbers and mega-churches, but it is still losing the battle for the culture. Minority groups who have mobilized their people in strategic ways are shaping the agenda in our nations even though they are smaller in numbers. The church must recognize its failure. We can't continue with "business as usual." We must unite together and return to a truly biblical model of discipling nations.

While denominations and independent churches have legitimate and honest differences of theology that may not allow them to build churches together, it should not prevent us from uniting for the good of our communities. It is possible to maintain our liturgical preferences while also uniting behind our common biblical worldview to fulfill the great commission mission and to disciple our nations. Without this type of unity, we will surely fail.

The place where this should begin is locally. Throughout history Christians were influential nationally in each of the seven areas of culture, but it started at the local level first. Many Christian efforts never get off the ground because of a mistaken notion that someone has to start things nationally before we can do anything locally. In reality, the local groups have the real power to shape history. Only when change is happening locally is it possible to connect regionally and nationally in a meaningful way.

Many organizations tend to start top down in an effort to create one organization that is identified with one leader or brand. This is a mistake. As soon as the enemy is able to demonize and stigmatize that leader or group, the movement stops being effective. No, in order to truly outlast the opposition, we must build local and diverse organizations. If one group is targeted and stereotyped negatively by the opponents of our values, then let it die and work through a new group which may have gained favor in the community. Jesus diversified by sending them out two by two, rather than as one top-down, monolithic group. And Paul said it does not matter who sows, who waters and who reaps (1 Cor 3:7,8). This is the way to win—with a mindset that is focused on the advancement on God's kingdom rather than our own personal organizations.

As we begin to work with a long-term, strategic plan, there are five key steps we can take to see this transformation take place, starting at the local level:

1. Provide *general education* in the discipling nations transformation vision

In each local community, we need more of the Christian community to learn about Christ's truly great commission to disciple nations, in order to mobilize believers beyond merely winning souls for heaven and building churches. Good organizations may exist already in the community that can help in this general educational step. Pastors also should be equipped to train their congregations in a Biblical understanding of discipling nations.

2. Identify and provide *advanced training* for leaders in all five signs discussed in this book and the seven related cultural institutions.

In each local community, we need to give general education on discipling nations, but we also need to provide advanced training for leaders in the seven spheres of society. It's not enough to simply be motivated but then go out with an un-renewed mind. We have to have in-depth teaching available on the local level (ideally in every local church to some degree) on the biblical best practices and worldview principles for each of the seven spheres of influence. Again, good organizations already exist that can help with this advanced training step. Most pastors may not feel adequate to do so, but can network with other teaching ministries to help supplement their church's basic discipleship.

3. Connect trained leaders in these professional fields into *networked teams*

Many churches are already completing the first two steps or can easily fit them into their discipleship programs. This third step though involves stepping out of our comfort zones to network with believers who are working in the seven areas of cultural influence. This may be challenging and seem quite radical for some churches and individuals, but it is a key to bringing transformation. In each of the seven areas of influence, there are many Christians who are working in their chosen professions but are largely limited in their impact because they are acting independently of each other. In each local community, we can identify those Christians who are already working in each area and begin to connect them in networks and teams that can work together to begin to influence their area of society. Some professional networks and Christian fellowship groups for businessmen, teachers, health care workers, and other professions already exist. No group has to yield to another or dissolve. Each is important. However, it is critical that we network together and be willing to embrace the idea of strategic planning and action. No organization has to lose its purpose and identity in this process. Rather, networking together helps every organization to be more well-known and effective, not less.

4. Execute long-term *strategic action plans for each of these professional fields.*

Another key but often overlooked step is the creation of long-term strategic plans for each of the seven cultural teams or networks mentioned above. Each of these teams must integrate their plans into a comprehensive city-wide plan (and later a national plan). Even in the rare occurrence today of a Christian city-wide transformation effort, it is almost overwhelmingly focused on prayer events, fellowship, and short-term and defensive plans rather than long-term offensive action plans. Real transformation in nations over the past 2000 years has only occurred when there has been intentional steps taken by the unified local church to get Christian leaders into the critical positions in the influential institutions of society.

Many times Christians have gotten elected to high office or been elevated to leadership positions in media or medicine, for example, but have been largely ineffective because of a lack of a strategic plan and network to help them execute it. The rare Christian leader at a high position is eventually discouraged or compromised in some way by the constant pressure of the opposition and temptation against him.

Success is absolutely dependent on a long-term strategy to raise up an entire movement of biblically trained leaders in the seven cultural areas that will rise to key positions through the recommendations and advocacy of Christian networks. This process takes time for individuals to earn experience, as well as credentials from institutions that the world respects, not just the church, and prove themselves worthy of higher positions. But within just twenty or thirty years it is possible for a young leader to become a top government official, banker, Hollywood producer, Hospital administrator, professor, television producer, news anchor, or even CEO or owner of a major company. When Christian leaders with a Biblical worldview and a vision to apply Biblical best practices to their sphere of influence rise to such places of authority, real transformation can begin to happen.

For this to be possible city-wide strategic Christian networks must develop plans to be at the top of those institutions in at least 20 years, and then must create real benchmarks, goals, and plan of work to make it happen. Then instead of focusing our unified efforts on reacting to pagan initiatives, we will begin to shape the trajectory of our communities in ways that have real meaning and lasting significance.

For pastors this may mean allowing their best people to sow their time and efforts into community institutions rather than solely in church activities. It may mean accepting the reality that they must send their best people to places like Wall Street or Hollywood or Harvard or Washington (or whatever is the equivalent of those in other nations) to gain credibility and be raised up to change the power bases of the culture and to affirm young leaders in this vision and calling.

This of course means being willing to work hard for changes that we may not see or enjoy in our own lifetime, but with the hope that our children or grandchildren will enjoy its fruit.

5. Develop *funding* for permanent *institutions in these professional fields*

There is rarely big transformation without a concurrent plan for sustainable funding of the strategic plan. A good plan for local and national transformation will not rely solely on donations but will develop a business model for making it financially-self-sustaining. This is why it is essential for local networks to incorporate all of the seven cultural team plans so that leaders from every sector of the community can see where the needs are and how entrepreneurs and businessmen can use their skills to help fulfill it. It is amazing how much money is made available from the very Christian businessmen who no longer feel that excited about simply another church facility that sits largely empty most of the week. These same business leaders get excited with the prospect that they can help create real institutions that change the world - new hospitals or movie studios or universities or political parties.

Concluding Thoughts:

Certainly, as local networks develop and grow, opportunities will arise to work in coordination with other cities in the region and state, and even nationwide. This leads to constant enrichment and development of regional and national strategy that can have truly historical impact.

Christian leaders must articulate this vision and for local strategic planning groups in each community and set long-term goals. Share it with the next generation and incorporate young leaders into the steering committee so that it does not die with the original organizers of the strategic plan. It must be multi-generational and long-term in order to work.

As the Pilgrims who arrived on the barren shores of America in 1620, we must recognize that we are but as "stepping stones unto others for so great a work." Those Christian Pilgrims were faithful and laid a foundation for the United States to bless the world for many years. Today, America needs new Pilgrims, and every nation needs the same.

Visionaries all over the world are arising in recent years with this dream. Most have yet to hear of them. The news is dominated by stories that seem to indicate the world is getting worse, but a powerful new undercurrent is already flowing. We mention some of them in this five-part book series – a new Christian party governing Latvia, millions of new home-schooled children in America, new medical leaders in Poland, new reconciliation leaders in South Africa, new media leaders in El Salvador, new universities in South Korea, new Christian governors and Senators in Indonesia and Colombia.

Many more untold efforts also are emerging. The fruit of their work will surely come but perhaps in the next generation. Don't be impatient and short in your vision. And it doesn't matter what your eschatology is. Even if one thinks Jesus is going to return very soon, He has never changed His commission to us. Occupy until He returns (Luke 19:13)! Go and disciple the nations!

APPENDIX

A Self-Assessment for Leaders

Two millennia of church history shows that revival and church growth alone can never fully transform a nation. Only when church leaders strategically focus on raising up leaders for society, are nations changed. The seven key areas or spheres of cultural influence are the battlefields where the war for our culture will be won or lost. A truly discipled nation is one where Biblical principles are being taught in all seven areas and where networks of support and strategic coordination are established for this purpose.

In Mark 16, the parallel passage to the Great Commission where Jesus added "signs" that would follow us, he provided a way to measure the church's progress in discipling nations. While Church is itself one of the seven key influential spheres of a nation, its mission is especially to disciple and equip leaders for the other six areas. Therefore, church leadership needs to create an intentional plan to accomplish this. A checklist is provided on the next page to help church leaders to assess their progress in this and develop a plan. It is a suggested list of "kingdom practices" rooted in the Bible that are effective in transforming culture. The list on the next page is not exhaustive by any means, but we hope that it will be used to stimulate your thinking and serve as a launching pad for your own strategic plans.

Are the five "Signs" of the Great Commission evident in your area?:
Is your church or larger Christian community intentionally providing ongoing teaching, mentoring & action opportunities in the following areas? Check off each item already existing in your community and a check if you or your congregation is actively connecting your people into them. If not, set a date to investigate it. See next page.

Cast Out the Nation's Demons

	My church?	Community?
Community-oriented Unified Prayer	_____	_____
Outward-oriented Apostolic Evangelism	_____	_____
Pastor that equip for community leadership	_____	_____

*List one short-term idea or potential project:*_____

Speak the Nation's New Tongues

Home & Church-based schools for children	_____	_____
Advanced worldview Education/Universities	_____	_____
Arts, Media and Entertainment	_____	_____

*List one short-term idea or potential project:*_____

Take Up the Nation's Serpents

Limiting Government via constitutions	_____	_____
voting, campaigning, advising	_____	_____
protest, flight, self-defense	_____	_____

*List one short-term idea or potential project:*_____

Drink the Nation's Deadly Things

Work, Business and Trade to increase wealth	_____	_____
Saving and Coordinated Christian Banking	_____	_____
Coordinated Giving and Caring for the Poor	_____	_____

*List one short-term idea or potential project:*_____

Lay Hands on the Nation's Sick

Doctors and Nurses Teaching & Care	_____	_____
Emergency Relief after disasters/Development	_____	_____
Reconciliation and Healing of Divisions	_____	_____

*List one short-term idea or potential project:*_____

The Global Transformation Network

In the 2000 years of church history many examples show where Christians had a huge impact in transforming their nations. Unfortunately much of that has stopped happening in modern times due to a narrowing of their mission to simply winning souls and growing churches. But many are aware that the modern church is losing the culture and that we must return to a truly biblical model that the historic church applied to disciple nations in 7 areas: politics, business, education, medicine, media, church and family. This vision is long-term, strategic and proven to succeed.

5 steps that our Transformation Network does in each nation:

1. Provide *general education* in the 5 signs Transformation vision
2. Identify and provide *advanced training* for 5 signs leaders
3. Connect trained 5 signs leaders into *networked teams*
4. Execute long-term *strategic 5 signs action plans*
5. Develop *funding* for permanent 5 signs *institutions*

In the next decade our vision is to have a strategic network working in every major city and nation around the globe.

These networks will have annual regional and national transformation summits to gather the leaders of each local network for encouragement and sharing of expertise. A national team will provide ongoing coaching and assistance to the leaders in different cities and will develop and provide a Transformation Toolbox with books, dvds, podcasts, and internet online courses. These national leaders will also be able to connect with others from different nations in their region of the world who are doing similar things and facing similar problems.

Contact the Global team to find out how to join or start *a network in your area*

We already serve over 40 nations. Contact us and tell us if you have interest or expertise in one or more of the 7 areas. If you have leadership gifts, we are looking for people to help create and facilitate local transformation teams. Go to our webpage at **www.NationalTransformation.com** (Espanol: www.TransformacionGlobal.com**)** or look for Global Transformation Network on **facebook**. You may also contact via email at NationalTransformation@gmail.com

Recommended Resources:

National Transformation by Dr. Mark Beliles is a 200 page book that gives an overview of the hand of God in the history of nations, and then introduces the seven key spheres of influence.

Christ's Strategy to Disciple Nations is a five-part series of books that gives historically-proven best practices for the church to transform society. The five titles in the series are:

How Nations Cast Out their Demons
How Nations Speak their New Tongues
How Nations Take up their Serpents
How Nations Drink their Deadly Things
How Nations Lay Hands on their Sick

To order these and many other books, dvds and online resources go to www.NationalTransformation.com
Or (Espanol: www.TransformacionGlobal.com**)**

Mark Beliles Biographical Information

Dr. Mark A. Beliles is president of the Global Transformation Network (www.NationalTransformation.com) and it's USA branch called the America Transformation Company (www.AmericaTransformationCompany.com) that identifies, coaches and connects leaders in key spheres of culture such as government, business, schools, churches and media. Beliles is a popular speaker and cultural leadership coach who has traveled to over 60 countries and addressed parliaments and high-level leaders of nations on the topic of faith and freedom. South African members of parliament have given to Beliles official tokens of recognition for his contribution to their successful transition away from apartheid. Beliles also serves as the North American facilitator in the global Transform World 2020 movement and one of the leaders of the Reconciled Church, the 4-14 Window, and other movements.

He founded an educational ministry called the Providence Foundation in 1983 and its Biblical Worldview University, and co-authored other books for popular audiences such as *America's Providential History* and *Contending for the Constitution:* Recalling the Christian Influence on the Writing of the Constitution and the Biblical Basis of American Law and Liberty, and *Liberating the Nations* and several other books just for international audiences.

Beliles, an ordained minister since 1977, has served as pastor of various non-denominational churches for over 35 years and was the founder of Grace Covenant Church in Charlottesville, Virginia. He has provided apostolic oversight to dozens of churches in the U.S. and abroad and today serves on the Apostolic Council of the International Communion of Evangelical Churches (presiding Bishop Harry Jackson). Beliles earned his Ph.D. from Whitefield Theological Seminary.

He has organized, with sponsorship of the Virginia Foundation for the Humanities, several scholarly symposiums held at the University of Virginia on Jefferson and religion that each featured dozens of nationally-known Jefferson scholars and church and state historians. He has served for many years as Chairman of the Charlottesville Historic Resources Committee and co-chairman of the city's 250th Anniversary observed in 2012. Beliles' most recent scholarly books on Thomas Jefferson are *Doubting Thomas?-The Religious Life and Legacy of Thomas Jefferson* and *The Selected Religious Letters and Papers of Thomas Jefferson.* (Books available at www.AmericaPublications.com)

He and his wife Nancy homeschooled their three children and now are blessed with eight grandchildren.

Printed in Great Britain
by Amazon

38583791R00067